outdoor feasts

outdoor feasts

Hugo Arnold

photography by

For Sue, with all my love

Acknowledgements

My thanks to Kyle, for suggesting, commissioning and editing *Outdoor Feasts* with such a gentle and understanding hand. My father, for teaching me that discovering a good picnic site requires effort, luck and more than a little dedication. My mother, who made me realise early on that no good outdoor feast is ever thrown together.

Thanks also go to my agent Jacqueline Korn at David Higham. Rosemary Stark, for her help, advice and encouragement which was invaluable. Anna Wright and Andrew Colls, whose hospitality and kindness were endless during our week shooting the pictures in the garden of their beautiful house. Justin Canning, for assisting and eating with unbridled keeness. Jill James, food and drink editor at the *Financial Times*, who originally commissioned the series on picnics. Robert Updegraff, for his inspiring design.

I particularly want to thank Georgia Glynn Smith, who took the photographs for this book. Her understated, natural approach to food photography has been a revelation to me. Gone were the hours spent setting things up, the bags of props usually hired to create a scene in food photography. Her wit, charm and enthusiasm all show through in her wonderful photographs.

First published in Great Britain in 1998 by
Kyle Cathie Ltd • 20 Vauxhall Bridge Road • London SW1V 2SA

ISBN 1 85626 284 7

Text © 1998 Hugo Arnold • Photography © 1998 Georgia Glynn Smith • Book Design © 1998 Kyle Cathie Ltd

Hugo Arnold is hereby identified as the author of this work in accordance with Section 77 of the Copyright, Designs and Patents Act 1988.

A CIP catalogue record for this title is available from the British Library.

Designed by Robert Updegraff • Printed and bound in Singapore by Kyodo Printing Co (Singapore) Pte Ltd

contents

Introduction

I am passionate about eating outside. Fresh air, the warmth of the sun on my back and the gentle rustle of trees all help to sharpen the senses. How well the wine tastes, how much more delicious is the bread, the fleshy, sun-rich olives and the moist, golden-yellow, mayonnaise-laden salmon sandwiches. If there is a lake or bubbling brook nearby, so much the better. It is time to relax. There is no better way to eat.

I have picnicked all my life. Childhood memories are full of swimming on deserted Irish beaches and in empty lakes and rivers before lunches of my mother's rough country pate, fiery radishes from the garden, French bread and stone-stoppered bottles of cider. Home-grown tomato salads and strong Canadian cheddar were the preface to seemingly endless bars of chocolate. We would then while away the afternoon, which seemed to stretch for ever under clear blue skies, before packing up the car and heading home. In reality of course, rain often threatened play, but nobody seemed to notice.

These days I'm more likely to be found picnicking in a London park, or my own back garden. On holiday, I will go to ridiculous lengths to find the perfect picnic spot, much to my wife's amusement (although thankfully she is always as enthusiastic as me).

Finding the site is all part of the ritual of a good picnic. The uncertainty, the sheer pleasure on those occasions when everything falls magically into place are what make picnics so wonderful. How glorious when you sit overlooking some raging torrent tumbling its way through a wooded valley, or better still find a pool deep and warm enough to swim in. Alternatively you chance upon a lush and green cowpat-free meadow with the sun kept at bay in the dappled shade of an ancient oak tree, or the golden empty beach, the sea racing to change colour as the clouds skip by in the midst of a late-summer storm.

But locating the site can be a hell of a job, the field is never where it used to be, the lake has moved and the view never had those pylons in before. And looking for somewhere new? The map, if there is one - mine is usually still sitting, neatly folded on the kitchen table back home - is never detailed enough or the factory not marked, the mountain grown. It's a frustrating business. I never leave enough time for this important consideration and there is a sense of rising panic as I think of all this delicious food and look at the car park and overflowing litter bins. "Surely we can find somewhere better than this," I tell myself, stifling the overwhelming sense of disappointment.

If I can barbecue so much the better, but the feast can be nothing more than a few rounds of thickly cut ham sandwiches laced with creamy, peppery mustard and alongside a bottle or two of beer. In summer there is everything to recommend the grand outdoor feast; cold poached salmon and wobbly mayonnaise, olive oil rich salads of deep red tomatoes, sweet roasted peppers and crisp green salad leaves. Bread with crunch, but also with enough softness to mop up delicious, garlic-influenced dressings. Cheese needs to have punch, nothing too subtle for the great outdoors and when it gets to the time for sweet things, something simple, a fruit salad or fool and lots of chocolate (quantity is important).

In an age when buying a ready-made outdoor feast has never been more convenient, it is easy to overlook how simple so many picnic foods are to prepare yourself. Taramasalata can be whipped up to a sea-fresh smoothness in minutes. Pale, nutty houmous, made from a can of chickpeas far outstrips any shop-bought tub. Succulent cold poached chicken is one of the classics and leaves the cook with a most delicious stock. Chilled refreshing soups, robust vegetable purees, tarts and pies with golden pastry crusts and rich, satisfying fillings. A bought plastic-wrapped sandwich just doesn't compare. If a barbecue is to hand, the making of hamburgers takes moments. Sausages even less time - and I'm not suggesting you make your own from scratch. Buy from a good butcher and spend your time on the mustardy things to accompany, a few salads and some decent bread.

With outdoor eating it pays to keep a handle on things. Designer canapes and the great outdoors are seldom compatible, but plenty of things are: spicy samosas, crunchy crostini and tortillas stuffed with enough deliciousness to ooze everywhere as you eat. The delicate parfait and iced mousse are for another time, another place. An outdoor feast needs strong robust flavours, dishes that don't mind the odd bump or two and can stand up to the great outdoors.

The back garden is a favourite spot, a time to indulge in primitive roasting, either over a barbecue, or in the dying embers of a bonfire. Baked sweet potatoes, the chilli butter melting to a rich and delicious mushiness. Or entrecote steak sizzling to a moist pink doneness. And then there are all the vegetables, meaty aubergine, blackened rich red peppers, fennel with its glorious aniseed kick and char-grilled smokiness.

Not all outdoor eating needs the heat of the sun. A slice of game pie and steaming mug of soup can make the most fantastic autumn feast. Sausage sandwiches and warming glasses of whisky to accompany fireworks. Or bowls of chilli to keep the heat of late summer alive on a cold evening when you are determined to eat outside, jumper-wrapped, for the last time.

This book covers food to prepare in the kitchen and take outside as well as cooking outdoors, which for most of us means a barbecue. Outdoors can mean a picnic, but I have also tried to cover those occasions when you are eating in the garden, or close by. Close enough, at any rate, to carry food.

Quantities

Working out how many people a recipe is likely to serve is possibly the hardest thing to predict. Fresh air increases appetites amazingly. Recipes in this book assume a fairly healthy appetite and that a given dish will be eaten with others.

Occasional feasts

Some of my favourite outdoor feasts have undoubtedly been ones where there was no real overall plan. Where people turn up with liquid and solid allsorts and despite the chaotic approach you end up eating and drinking well and more importantly having a very enjoyable time. How much does this have to do with the food? And how much the balmy weather, the idyllic, evening-sun drenched location, being surrounded by friends and family. Circumstance can count for a lot.

A few ideas for those occasions when circumstance is something you are reluctant to rely on.

Serious feasting

If numbers are large, keep it simple and make enough time to enjoy it yourself. The following is the menu from my mother's 60th birthday, a feast eaten on a perfect English summer's day in Sussex by 15 members of the family. We started with sushi, which everyone ate while chatting beforehand, and then continued with the following

Roasted red pepper and anchovy salad
Poached guinea fowl, summer vegetable and black olive salad with aioli
Summer pudding

Sunday lunch for 30 in the garden (with an additional 15 small children) when we moved house was the largest outdoor feast I had ever done.

It was a boiling hot day, but cocktail sausages with pots of mustard proved just the thing to keep everyone happy, particularly the younger guests. Bruschetta and crostini topped with all the variations given on page 22 were handed round with drinks before we all sat, French style, at an improvised trestle table running the length of the garden. The lamb and aubergine stew had been cooked the day before. Helpful guests - I always put guests to work if they offer - chopped vegetables and herbs for the couscous. The yoghurt with roasted cumin seeds, red onion and coriander was made in minutes. Green salads were placed in bowls along the length of the table. Everyone helped themselves to raspberries, strawberries and buckets of whipped cream and by 8pm those of us remaining started all over again.

Family picnics

For several years we have had a family holiday in the west of Ireland where my mother comes from. There is a lake in a forgotten corner of County Roscommon with a late-Georgian ruined house I have wanted to live in since the day I first saw it. If the weather allows, we arrive in time for swimming in what is the silkiest, softest water I know and then sit in the glorious Irish sunshine. Our picnic changes, but this is a favourite collection

Maldon's sea salt and freshly ground black pepper
Hard-boiled eggs
Home made mayonnaise as well as Hellmann's
A roast chicken
Sausages, wrapped in tin foil and still warm if possible
Tomatoes, shallots, fresh basil and extra virgin olive oil
White and red wine, beer and water, all in the chill box
Sticks of French bread
Bars of chocolate, also in the chill box

I have yet to go to Glyndeborne, but my picnic, if we are ever lucky enough to get there, will probably go something like this:

Smoked salmon, capers, extra virgin olive oil and brown bread
Crab mayonnaise, mixed leaf salad and cold new potatoes
St Felicien cheese
Fresh strawberries sprinkled with a little very ancient balsamic vinegar

Have food, will travel, but what with?

Not for me the designed hamper, sets of this, racks of that. The numbers never fit, there are five of us feasting not four, my cold curry lacks a receptacle and there isn't room for the bread anyway. Battered baskets, wearing wounds from previous campaigns, hold plastic tubs and oodles of tin foil - it may be old-fashioned, but there is something so up-to-the-minute about its space-age shininess, its hi-fi crinkle and crackle - and greaseproof paper. Classic wrapping of the best kind, although cling-film has its uses.

Basket handles are important, as is the shape, wide at the bottom, narrower at the top, my hands cannot stretch across a great divide. My picnic basket has a used-and-abused quality to it and I like it that way.

Pack sparingly and bear in mind how many of you there are. Nobody should be empty handed and no basket too full. Spread the load.

Mismatching cutlery bound with a rubber band stops it rattling and napkins separate plates for safety and convenience making serving easier. Napkins at table are a nicety, on picnics they are essential. Paper ones too, for the inevitable mopping up.

Plastic containers with good seals are hard to beat, nobody wants to be landed with the job of scooping your delicious cold ratatouille from the depths of a rough-woven basket. And they weigh little.

Polystyrene cups should stay in the office, unless there is hot soup, when they have their uses, although soup from a wide open plate, or mug definitely tastes better. Wine, beer lemonade, all taste better from glass.

Tarts should be left in their tart tins until you arrive, the metal will protect the edges. Salads should not meet their dressings until you are ready to eat them, or wilting sets in. Remember a bowl, plastic may suffer on the beauty side, but think of the weight.

If any male among the party says he will bring his new penknife so don't worry about a corkscrew, ignore him. A second one won't spoil the party and too often the new penknife fails to turn up.

Cool boxes were a wonderful invention, it's a shame they couldn't make eternal ice blocks because I'm forever forgetting to put mine in the freezer. Make sure everything going in is cold, bottles respond well to a last 30-minute boost in the freezer. If you fill up the space with warm items it only serves to increase the overall temperature. If a cool box is not available a freezer-boosted bottle of wine lasts for an hour or so wrapped thickly in newspaper.

Salt and pepper. For my money essential. The salt has to be Maldon's and pepper comes in a pepper mill, to be ground freshly, not dusted from a container.

What to sit on?

Picnic tables have their place, although forest sites have a lead over lay byes, by a long way. I favour a light table hauled from the boot of the car along with a deck chair or two, but with larger numbers this is out of the question. Rugs are the only answer when numbers are large. And you need lots of them. Too frequently I unload the food on to the one available rug only to realise that with the pots of mustard, onion tart, cold roast beef and salads there is now nowhere for anyone to sit.

Picnic checklist

Salt and pepper
Cutlery, not your best and who's looking if it doesn't match
Plates, paper at a pinch, depends how far you have to walk
Bowls for salads, plastic unless you have staff to carry them
Serving spoons
A sharp knife and small chopping board
Corkscrew and bottle opener
Glasses, stemmed tend to fall over
Napkins, linen and paper
Rug(s) once you've laid out the food it's amazing how little room is left for people
Mustard of various kinds – people are fussy about mustard
Mayonnaise, homemade for preference, although my wife says Hellmann's is better!
Gherkins (for pâté) – look for a good supplier, vinegar can spoil gherkins
Chutney (it's been sitting in the cupboard and who knows, somebody might like it?)
Chocolate, but don't bother too much about quality – it will all get wolfed anyway

Eating in the open
street food as finger food

Street foods from around the world, as near to instant food as I want to get, make excellent preliminaries to any outdoor feast. *Sushi* from Japan, *samosas* from India, *falafals* from the Middle East – these are the things to snack on while everyone settles down. Strong, robust flavours all wrapped up and ready to go. Guests relax, late-comers don't feel left out, children are happy and the elderly content. A glass of wine, a cold beer, a tumbler of fresh lemonade and things are already looking good.

Part of the joy of feasting outdoors for me is that there is less structure, more chance to stroll through the offerings at will. Plates piled high with everything, or delicately arranged with one or two choice items, depending on your wish. But when to start is crucial. Women and children may come first in a nautical emergency, but at a feast everyone stands on equal ground.

I can't hold back. I want to, but food outdoors has an eat-me-now attitude that is always irresistible. Too often, being a greedy soul, I dive in to scoop up the first serving of taramasalata, the first slice of terrine only to find the feast-maker, often the unpacker too, has an entirely different order of procedure in mind. A few sun-dried tomatoes – Sicilian style – perhaps, or a sausage roll, wrapped lovingly in greaseproof paper and foil to keep it warm. There I stand feeling embarrassed, the wrong food heading mouthwards with so much speed it is all I can do to halt proceedings.

Any outdoor feast needs a beginning, a point at which those participating know they can join in without feeling they have started too early. Sitting on a rug under an oak tree deep in some forest glade, or even at a makeshift table in the garden, you need morsels you can pick up and eat without effort and this is where the culinary ragbag of the world has gems to offer. After all, in another land, it's just a snack to be grabbed on the way. Following are a few favourites.

Caponata with Toasted Pine Nuts and Ciabatta

SERVES 4-6

800g/1lb 12oz aubergine, cubed
olive oil
1 onion, peeled and finely
  chopped
3 sticks celery, trimmed and
  finely chopped
400g/14oz tin chopped
  tomatoes
1 tablespoon sugar
125ml/4fl oz red wine vinegar
½ cup capers, rinsed well
75g/3oz pitted green olives,
  roughly chopped
1 heaped tablespoon pine nuts
2 loaves (or 1 large one) of
  ciabatta bread

Caponata epitomises Sicilian food; great vegetables, given a simple treatment which somehow renders them so much greater than the sum of their parts. Perhaps it is because Sicilian vegetables are so wonderful, strong in both colour and flavour. Hard not to be I suppose with that intense Mediterranean sun. The sweet and sour element from the sugar and vinegar suggests a mediaeval influence. Wherever it comes from, what results is a gloriously rich concoction that seeps into slices of ciabatta like butter into mash.

• Combine the aubergine with a generous dollop of olive oil in a bowl and toss so the aubergine is well coated. Grill until golden brown, if the aubergine becomes slightly charred, so much the better.

• Sauté the onion for 10 minutes in 3 tablespoons of olive oil without colouring. Add the celery and continue to sauté for a further 5 minutes. Add the tomatoes, lower the heat and cook for a further 15 minutes.

• Combine the sugar and vinegar in a saucepan and bring to the boil. Add the capers and green olives and stir into the tomato mixture along with the aubergine. Cook gently for 5 minutes and then remove from the heat.

• Lightly toast the pine nuts under the grill or in a dry frying pan and sprinkle over the caponata. Allow to cool and serve with large slices of the ciabatta. The longer caponata is left to sit the better the flavours become. It will keep in the fridge for several days, but should be served no colder than room or outdoor temperature. Tightly boxed, it will transport perfectly in a rucksack, and taste all the better when you open it.

Vegetable Samosas with Coriander Chutney and Red Onion Relish

MAKES 20 SAMOSAS

1 dessertspoon mustard seeds
juice of 1 lemon
2 tablespoons vegetable oil, plus
    enough for deep frying
1 onion, peeled and finely
    chopped
200g/7oz defrosted frozen peas
2.5cm/1in cube of fresh ginger,
    grated
cayenne pepper
500g/1lb cooked potato, diced
bunch coriander, roughly
    chopped
1 teaspoon cumin seeds
225g/8oz shortcrust pastry

CORIANDER CHUTNEY

1 bunch of fresh coriander,
    picked and roughly chopped
pinch of cayenne pepper
2 tablespoons vegetable oil
salt and pepper

RED ONION RELISH

1 red onion, peeled and thinly cut
    into half-moon slices
1 dessertspoon salt
a little olive oil
1 dessertspoon finely chopped
    parsley

I spent a year travelling in India and samosas *became both everyday breakfast and anytime snacks. Whenever a bus or train stopped, street vendors would storm the passengers with ice-cream, soft drinks,* samosas *and tea. I can still remember the taste of that sweet, stewed tea and* samosas *after an overnight trip – the perfect breakfast crouched by the roadside watching hundreds if not thousands push their bicycles to work or transport entire families on Vespas.*

The stuffing can vary, depending on your preference, but spiced potato and minced meat are the most traditional. For more formal home consumption, samosas *make a good first course, smarter when served on top of a generous and well dressed salad.*

Traditionally samosas *are made from an oil-based pastry but shortcrust will do; they are deepfried, but I must confess I don't much like deepfrying. As an alternative, you can brush oil over the pastry and bake in a preheated oven, at 200°C/400°F/Gas Mark 6.*

• Combine the mustard seeds and lemon juice and set aside. Heat the vegetable oil in a frying pan and sauté the onions for 5 minutes. Add the peas, ginger and a generous pinch of cayenne pepper. Sauté for a further 2 minutes before adding 2 tablespoons of water. Cover and simmer until the peas are cooked. Stir in the potatoes and coriander.

• Toast the cumin seeds in a hot dry frying pan until lightly coloured and add to the potato mixture, along with the mustard seeds and lemon juice. Season with salt and pepper and set aside.

• Divide the pastry into 10 balls and cover all but 1 with cling film. Roll the remaining ball out to a disk about 15cm/6in in diameter, cut in half and roll each half up to form a cone. Seal the edge with a little water and place a little of the potato mixture in the cone, fold over the top and seal with water. Repeat with the remaining 9 balls.

• Heat about 5cm/2in of vegetable oil in a pan and when hot, add the samosas in a single layer and fry, turning as they brown. Serve with the coriander and red onion relish.

Coriander chutney

Combine the coriander, cayenne pepper and oil, season with salt and pepper and serve.

Red onion relish

Combine the onion and salt in a sieve, mix well and leave to drain over a cup or bowl for 10 minutes. Rinse well under plenty of cold water to remove the salt, pat dry and toss with a little oil and the parsley. Serve.

Falafals with Minted Yoghurt

SERVES 4

300g/10oz dried skinned broad
   beans (available from health
   food shops)
3 garlic cloves, peeled
2 tablespoons shallots, roughly
   chopped
1 bunch of parsley
1 teaspoon ground cumin
pinch of cayenne pepper
salt and pepper

vegetable oil, for deep frying

300ml/10fl oz thick yoghurt
2 bunches of mint, finely
   chopped

In Beirut, falafal shops are everywhere, an import from Egypt that has become an integral part of Lebanese cuisine. Fast food joints where the buy-to-go approach is loosely interpreted, many of the customers hovering in the shop as they munch their way through a falafal sandwich. No two slices of white with a beanburger in between here though. What you get is a disc of Lebanese bread, thin and full-flavoured. Into its centre go two or three falafals, along with a few pickles, some tomatoes and delicately coloured pink radish as well as tarratur (tahini, thinned down with water and lemon juice). Elegantly rolled up with a paper sleeve, it's one of the neatest sandwiches I have seen anywhere. If not served in a sandwich, then falafals handed round in common-or-garden Tupperware with this minted yoghurt is my preferred option. You can make falafals either with dried broad beans, or chickpeas, or a mixture of the two.

• Soak the broad beans overnight. Drain and combine in a food processor with all the other falafal ingredients, season with salt and pepper and blitz to a purée.

• With a spoon dipped in water, form the purée into squashed balls about 2.5cm/1in in diameter. Deep fry in the vegetable oil until golden.

• Combine the yoghurt and mint, season with salt and pepper and serve with the falafals at room temperature.

Boreks

SERVES 4

1 onion, peeled and finely
   chopped
olive oil
225g/8oz minced steak
squeeze of tomato purée
2 bunches of parsley, finely
   chopped
1 egg
salt and pepper
225g/8oz filo pastry
melted butter, to seal
vegetable oil, for deep frying
bunch of mint leaves, finely
   chopped
juice of 1 lemon

Boreks are the Turkish version of an Indian samosa, Cornish pastie, or Moroccan bistilla. Parcels of something delicious made tiny for parties and celebrations and in a slightly larger model for everyday use. While a yeast dough is often used in Turkey, filo makes a fine substitute and has the added advantage of coming out of a packet. Not being one so dedicated to the art of pastry making that I want to get into making filo, packets are fine.

Feta makes a good vegetarian option with herbs and spices but I confess to a weakness for this meat version.

• Sauté the onion in 2 tablespoons of olive oil for 20 minutes without colouring. Add the meat and toss well so it loses its colour. Add the tomato purée, cook for 2 minutes and then add half the parsley. Remove from the heat and stir in the egg. Season and set this parcel stuffing aside.

• Using the filo pastry make parcels of your chosen size, sealing the ends with melted butter. Cigar and triangle shapes are traditional. For the cigars, cut a thin rectangle, place the filling at the short end, fold in the 2 long sides and roll up to seal. For the triangles, use a slightly wider and shorter rectangle and fold triangle on triangle until the pastry is used up, and then seal.

• Deep fry in vegetable oil until golden brown or alternatively brush with oil and bake in a preheated oven at 200°C/400°F/gas mark 6 for 10-15 minutes or until golden brown and crispy.

• Combine the mint leaves with the remaining parsley and enough olive oil to form a sauce. Season with salt and pepper and lemon juice and serve with the boreks at room temperature.

Sushi

There is an art to making sushi, and I haven't mastered it. I've watched the experts closely in the sushi bars of Tokyo, yet still my sushi ends up slightly uneven, slightly askew. My balance of rice to fish, of wasabi to fish, of rice to seaweed always seems out, but in the end I like it that way. I like too, the frustration of trying to roll seaweed around too much filling, of trying to ease the wasabi off the end of my chopstick, of coming across it as a burning lump in the middle of a mouthful, so I get all hot and bothered. I'm not good on sameness and uniformity, I like mess and

disorder, which is a good thing when you make sushi at home because it's hard to get it neat and tidy like those trays in the supermarkets, or the bars in Tokyo. Well-made sushi is food for the gods, but homemade is an enormous amount of fun, too.

There are two basic forms of sushi, nigiri (hand-formed) and maki (rolled). It is the maki which travels well. You need to use short-grain Japanese rice, its texture and stickiness being crucial. You can use other fish, like salmon or bass, but make sure it really is fresh.

SERVES 4

300g/10oz Japanese rice, rinsed in cold running water until the water is clear

1 dessertspoon caster sugar

2 tablespoons rice vinegar

400g/14oz tuna, filleted and trimmed

1 cucumber, peeled and deseeded

1 bunch spring onions

6 sheets nori seaweed

1 small jar of *keta* (salmon roe), lump fish or, if you are feeling flush, caviar

wasabi

soy sauce

• Combine the rice with 300ml/10floz of cold water, cover with a tight-fitting lid and bring to the boil. Reduce the heat and cook for 15 minutes. Remove from the heat and set aside still covered to steam for a further 12 minutes.

• Fluff up with a fork and if not quite cooked, return the lid and leave for a further 5 minutes. Dissolve the sugar in the vinegar and mix into the rice while it is still warm. Cover with a tea towel and set aside.

• Cut the tuna into strips and the cucumber and spring onion into thin strips. Lay a sheet of nori out on a dry tea towel. Spread a line of rice along its width leaving 5cm/2in clear at the bottom. The line should be about 1cm/2in wide and about 0.5cm/¼in high. Press down lightly with a chop stick to make an indent and place the tuna and keta on top.

• Dabble wasabi along its length and top with cucumber and spring onion. Fold over the bottom end of the nori and using the tea towel or straw mat gently but firmly roll up.

• Leave for 10 minutes to allow the nori to become moistened by the ingredients and then cut into 2.5cm/1in lengths. Serve with wasabi and soy sauce.

TOPPINGS

Tomato and garlic

At the height of summer, when garlic cloves are plump and juicy and tomatoes red and full-flavoured this is hard to better. Rub garlic on the grilled bread, dribble over olive oil and either top with roughly chopped tomatoes, or rub the cut side of a tomato into the bread. In Spain this latter technique is popular for breakfast with a coffee on the way to work.

Chicken livers, pine nuts and capers

olive oil; 1 onion, peeled and finely chopped; 400g/14oz chicken livers; 150ml/¼ pint dry white wine; 1 tablespoon capers, well rinsed; salt and pepper; 1 tablespoon pine nuts, lightly toasted in a dry frying pan. Heat 3 tablespoons of olive oil in a frying pan and sauté the onion for 10 minutes without colouring. Add the chicken livers and colour lightly on the outside, tossing so they are evenly cooked. Add the white wine and capers and season with pepper and salt (take care if you are using salted capers). Simmer for 5 minutes, or until the livers are cooked. Blitz briefly in a food processor, stir in the pine nuts and spread on the toast.

Wild mushrooms and garlic

800g/1lb 12oz fresh wild mushrooms; olive oil; 1 tablespoon finely chopped shallots; 1 garlic clove, peeled and finely chopped; 1 tablespoon finely chopped parsley; nutmeg; Parmesan. Sauté the mushrooms in 3 tablespoons of olive oil until wilted and tender, add the shallots and toss well. Add the garlic and parsley, cook for 1 minute and remove from the heat. Grate in a little nutmeg, stir and spoon on to slices of toast. Sprinkle over Parmesan and serve. If you cannot get fresh wild mushrooms, use the same quantity of field mushrooms and add 15g/½ oz dried wild mushrooms soaked for 20 minutes in a little hot water (add the water too).

Bruschetta and Crostini

Bruschetta and crostini both amount to much the same thing – things on toast. Crostini di formaggio may sound fashionable, but I'm equally enthusiastic about cheese on toast. The bread is crucial, it must be good quality country bread, sliced white is better left for the ducks, poor things.

Bruschetta is dry bread which is grilled, while crostini are oiled and then cooked, often in an oven – but also under a grill – which helps to crisp them up. Don't ever forget how much better they all taste when the bread is cooked on the barbecue. All that smoky, char-grilled taste infused with a full-flavoured bread is simple food at its best, you can almost forget about the topping.

While Bruschetta can be large in size, I tend to the view that crostini should be mouthful size, their tendency to break up can make for an awful mess on your picnic rug. Crostini can be cooked in advance, and will stay crisp for a day or two, Bruschetta on the other hand need to be grabbed while searingly hot from the barbecue, rubbed with garlic, liberally doused with olive oil and then topped, or not, with something delicious. Below are some favourites and a few suggestions; don't feel restricted however, the list really is endless.

Bruschetta: Cut slices of bread slightly thinner than usual. Place on the barbecue and cook until golden brown – a matter of seconds – repeat on the other side. Rub with a cut clove of garlic and dribble over a liberal quantity of olive oil. If the bread and oil are good, this makes a fantastic feast just by itself.

Crostini : I think French baguettes make the best. Slice on a slight diagonal, brush with oil and either grill until golden brown over the barbecue, or in a hot oven or under the grill. If you are using an oven it must be hot, a medium heat turns the bread into leather.

The olive oil: because the oil is cooked on the crostini there is little point in using anything particularly special. Not so with bruschetta, this is the time to break out the best cold pressed extra virgin estate bottled nectar you have been saving up. And don't hold back, if you're not licking it off your fingers you're missing out.

Lentils

2 tablespoons finely chopped shallots; 2 tablespoons olive oil; 1 chilli, deseeded and finely chopped; 1 250g/8oz tin Italian lentils (yes they are better), juice and zest of 1 lemon; 1 tablespoon finely chopped parsley; salt and pepper. Gently sauté the shallots in the olive oil for 5 minutes, add the chilli, cook for a further minute and then stir in the lentils. Stir well so everything is coated, remove from the heat and add the lemon juice and zest along with the parsley. Stir well and season to taste.

Other suggestions:

Tomato, mozzarella and anchovy
Roasted red pepper and anchovy (see recipe on page 134)
Sun dried tomatoes, roughly puréed with olive oil, Parmesan and garlic
Tapenade (see recipe on page 72)
Grilled vegetables (see recipe on page 111)
Goat's cheese and pine nuts
Cannellini beans with rosemary and red onion
Fresh grilled sardines
Grilled peaches, figs and pears on panettone with cinnamon and sugar

Yakitori

SERVES 4

75ml/3fl oz soy sauce
3 tablespoons rice vinegar
1 tablespoon caster sugar
4 tablespoons sake (or dry
   sherry)
2 star anise
2.5cm/1in piece of root ginger,
   roughly chopped
2 chicken breasts, skinned
400g/14oz beef fillet
skewers

The Japanese version of skewers and typically done in a smaller version. Not quite street food in that the eating is usually done in a bar in Japan, but the principle is the same – a snack, to be chased with a beer or sake and consumed on the way home from work. Chicken is the preferred ingredient but I got the lot when I was there, from breast meat to thigh, wing to leg, kidneys to livers, hearts to gizzards (the latter were particularly good). The cooking is done over charcoal, hence perfect for barbecues. In Japan, you can buy barbecues specially designed so the sticks rest on a bar either side of the heat which prevents them burning. A good soaking in water is a useful alternative, as is covering the ends with foil. This recipe is for chicken, but beef, pork and lamb also work well. If the idea of preparing the marinade doesn't appeal, a bottle of good quality Teriyaki marinade is a good substitute.

• Combine the first 6 ingredients in a saucepan with 5 tablespoons of water, bring to the boil and simmer for 20 minutes. Remove from the heat, allow to cool, strain and place in a bowl.

• Cut the meat into small cubes, thread onto skewers and leave to soak in the marinade for at least 30 minutes. Barbecue or grill, turning frequently, until cooked.

Frittata

SERVES 4

6 eggs
butter
salt and pepper

Where a traditional French omelette is supposedly light and airy, the point of frittata *is to exclude the air from the eggs. Firm, moist and flavoured with a whole host of different ingredients, it is an ideal traveller, never too badly affected by the odd bruise or bash. What goes in depends on how authentic you want to be. Grated cheese, or roughly chopped prosciutto are permitted, as are leftover pasta, courgettes and baby artichokes. Herbs are allowed, as is garlic. Less authentic, but to my mind pretty damn good, are ratatouille, lightly blanched broccoli or asparagus, grilled aubergine, the marinated mushrooms on page 126 and smoked salmon. The secret is not to use too much of the flavouring or you override the taste of the eggs. The latter must be the best quality and in tip-top shape. Stale eggs are better in the bin (if an egg stands up – that is pointed end up – in a glass of cold water it's time to go shopping).*

The quantity of eggs depends on numbers being fed, but I usually use 6 eggs to 4 people and add a few extra as new arrivals dictate – there is no hard and fast rule. You need a good, heavy bottomed pan. Combine your chosen flavouring with the stirred not shaken eggs, air bubbles are to be avoided – season with salt and pepper and pour into the pan when the butter is lightly frothing. Cook over the lowest heat until just set. Flash under a grill to firm up the top, allow to cool and serve.

To accompany? Some good bread, a lightly dressed salad perhaps. Best of all, however, is simply to eat a wedge with your fingers before any other food arrives.

Crudites

The street in this case is more likely to be a field or terrace in France somewhere for it is the French who excel at crudities. The attraction is speed. Prepared in advance, the vegetables and various accompaniments will satisfy children and adults alike while the rest of your feast is unpacked. Resist the urge to combine your chosen selection of vegetables, as the topsy turvy world of any journey tends to create a mess. Use a selection of small containers or better still a wide platter. Splashes of red radishes, green courgettes, yellow peppers, white fennel and black olives make a stunning start to any meal. Heaped in a disordered pile, they look, well, like a disordered pile. This is a picnic not a cocktail party. Matchsticks for the former, here you want batons. The less cutting up, the better everything will travel. You will need bread, and lots of it, to mop up the delicious dips below.

Carrots: young and organic are superb, a good scrub is all they need; celery: separate the sticks, trim and wash; cucumber: peel and deseed, a little salting (ie. 10 minutes) helps to concentrate the flavour but leave any longer and the salt takes over; fennel: trim and cut into wafer-thin slices; radishes: Trim and wash; tomatoes: quarter and deseed, removing the core as you go.

Dips to accompany: a good mustardy vinaigrette (page 157), mayonnaise (page 157), aioli (page 85), tzatiki (page 115), houmous, salsa verde (page 82), or tapenade (page 72).

Soups and Hearty Sandwiches

Sandwiches were made for eating outdoors. Portable, convenient and self-contained, they travel well. But it is not because of their co-operation that I adore them, a sandwich that behaves well is not welcome. I want the ingredients to spill out, to make a statement, all glistening and oozing between two firm slices of bread.

It is the Americans who have perfected the sandwich. Ordering one in a busy New York deli is one of life's great experiences. Which type of ham, which type of mustard, which type of bread, pickles, mayo, S&P, to go, to stay? So bamboozled was I the first time that I made the mistake of changing my mind to salt beef half way through ordering. The queue behind me was not pleased. What I got, however, was this mountain of spicy moist salt beef, pepper-sharp mustard, eye-watering horseradish, silky beetroot, crunchy coleslaw, salad and gherkins between two slices of sesame seed rye. I sat on a park bench and feasted for an age.

For me, since that experience in New York, a sandwich starts with the bread. Will it be rye, sourdough, black olive or perhaps a baguette. It might be ciabatta or focaccia, pitta or maybe even a muffin. A muffin is the perfect home for a fried egg and bacon, the whole wrapped in foil to be eaten on an early morning train with a flask of steaming coffee. No buffet car? No worries.

After the bread the fun really starts and my favourite sandwiches are the ones made with leftovers: the likes of cold ratatouille, with feta perhaps, or maybe some cold lamb. Cold curry, Indian cuisine's real secret, slips neatly into a warmed and split pitta to be eaten with a little yoghurt or some of that succulent leftover Indian pickle.

Gazpacho and vichyssoise are the fillet steak and Dover soles of chilled soups, classic and better left alone. For summer picnics I adore them both, particularly gazpacho.

But it is after the clocks go back that hot soups come into their own. Guy Fawkes night, when you are outside for the fireworks and everything is crisp, dry and freezing is transformed with cups of steaming soup – game with ginger and spring onions, or noodle with guinea fowl and mushroom – take your pick.

Chilled Chickpea and Chilli Soup with Mustard Seed and Tomato Relish

SERVES 4

750g/1lb 10oz chickpeas,
    soaked overnight
1 dessertspoon mustard seeds
juice and zest of 1 lime
2 tablespoons tahini
3 tablespoons olive oil
1 onion, peeled and finely
    chopped
1 chilli, peeled and finely
    chopped
2 garlic cloves, peeled and finely
    chopped
1 litre/1¾ pints chicken stock
salt and pepper
1 bunch of mint, picked over,
    washed and roughly chopped
juice and zest of 2 lemons
200g/7oz cherry tomatoes,
    roughly chopped
4 spring onions, trimmed and
    finely sliced

• Generously cover the chickpeas with cold water, bring to the boil, removing any scum that rises to the surface, lower the heat and simmer until tender. This can take anything from 40 minutes to 1½ hours, depending on the age of the peas. Drain, reserving the liquid and peas.

• Combine the mustard seeds with the juice and zest of the lime and set aside. Place the jar of tahini in a jug, pour over boiling water and set aside (this helps to liquefy the paste).

• Heat the olive oil in a large pan and sauté the onion for 10 minutes without colouring. Add the chilli and garlic, stir for 30 seconds and then add the cooked chickpeas and chicken stock. Season with salt and pepper. Bring to the boil and simmer for 15 minutes. Remove from the heat and stir in the tahini, mint, juice and zest of the lemons. Adjust the seasoning if necessary.

• Liquidise in batches to a smooth purée, pass through a conical sieve, cool and refrigerate. Alternatively, skip the sieve stage, depending on how smooth or coarse you like the soup.

• Combine the cherry tomatoes, spring onions and mustard seeds, lime juice and zest. Spoon the chilled chickpea soup into wide soup plates, cups or glasses and serve with a generous dollop of the relish in the middle.

Pea, Pancetta and Mint Soup

SERVES 6

4 tablespoons finely chopped shallots
3 tablespoons olive oil
2 slices pancetta, finely chopped
2 garlic cloves, peeled and finely chopped
750g/1lb 10oz peas
1 bunch of parsley, finely chopped
1.5 litres/2¾ pints light chicken stock
salt and pepper
1 bunch of mint, finely chopped

The pea is a curious vegetable in that it has no staying power once picked. As soon as the pod is removed from the plant the sugars start to convert to starch which, over time, mean the pea develops a woody flavour and loses all its sweetness. So much for the piles of fresh peas sitting in hoppers in supermarkets. It's for this reason that many restaurants prefer frozen peas. They are sweeter, more consistent and storable. Some cooks will still argue for the greater complexity of flavours in a fresh pea, but to my mind the crucial question is, just how fresh. If you have a garden, or comparable access to a supply of fresh peas, adding a dozen of the better looking pods adds a richness and body to the finished soup.

• Sauté the shallots in the olive oil for 5 minutes without colouring. Add the pancetta and, a minute later, the garlic and sauté for a further 2 minutes.

• Add the peas and parsley, coat in the oil and pour over the stock. Bring to the boil, season with salt and pepper, lower the heat and simmer for 3 minutes, or until the peas are tender.

• Liquidise to a purée and pass though a fine sieve. Chill and serve with a generous sprinkling of mint. A dollop of cream is traditional, but I prefer it without.

Chilled Broad Bean and Avocado Soup

SERVE 4

500g/1lb shelled broad beans
1 onion, peeled and finely chopped
3 tablespoons olive oil
1 garlic clove, peeled and finely chopped
1 litre/1¾ pints light chicken stock
1 bunch of parsley, leaves picked and stalks tied in a bundle
salt and pepper
1 ripe avocado
juice of 1 lemon
125ml/4fl oz whipping cream
1 bunch of coriander, picked and roughly chopped

The first time I proposed giving Sue, my wife, broad beans for dinner she curled her nose up in disgust and said they were one of the few things she couldn't stand, 'so bitter and rubbery'. Were we talking about the same thing I inquired? Pale green, with a delicate mealy flavour that made you think of bright summer days. Grey and bitter was the counter response. Surely some mistake I thought and so we shelled the beans, blanched them in water and started to remove the skins, much to Sue's amazement.

It is the skins, not the beans, that are bitter. They must, except on the youngest specimens, be thrown in the bin. After all that trouble you are left with one of the best things to come out of any vegetable garden. In Italy, they eat the first broad beans of the season with a little Parmesan to accompany, next comes the pasta with broad beans, pancetta and Parmesan and later on they are dried to be used in soups, stews and casseroles as well as being roasted with salt, a delicious alternative to peanuts.

• Blanch the beans in boiling water, drain, refresh with cold water and slide off and dscard the tough outer skin. Sauté the onion in the olive oil for 10 minutes without colouring. Add the garlic and beans, and continue cooking for 2 minutes.

• Pour over the stock and add the parsley stalks, bring to the boil, season with salt and pepper, lower the heat and simmer for 20 minutes, or until the beans are cooked. Allow to cool, blitz in a liquidiser and push through a sieve.

• Mash the avocado to a smooth paste with a fork and work in the lemon juice. Whip the cream, stir in the mashed avocado and the coriander and then stir into the broad bean mixture. Chill and serve in shallow bowls.

Hot Pumpkin Soup with Red Pepper Relish

SERVES 4-6

2kg/4½ lb pumpkin
4 tablespoons olive oil
2 onions, peeled and finely
   chopped
1 teaspoon ground coriander
2 teaspoons ground cumin
½ teaspoon ground turmeric
pinch of cayenne pepper
2.5cm/1-in cube ginger, peeled
   and roughly chopped
3 garlic cloves, peeled and
   finely chopped
1 litre/1¾ pints chicken stock
salt and pepper
1 roasted red pepper, peeled
a bunch of coriander, picked
   over and roughly chopped
1 dessertspoon toasted
   sesame seeds

Hollowed out for Halloween, its interior as often as not binned, the humble pumpkin gets a poor deal in my view. All that golden, sweet-tasting flesh makes the most wonderful soups and stews, not to mention pies and candies. That's if your pumpkin is up to it. Too often these huge Halloween specimens have contained a surfeit of water. But that is all changing. The supermarkets are coming round to the idea that big is not necessarily best, and that some of us want to do more to our pumpkins than sculpt a scary face. Look for the smaller specimens, where the sugars tend to be more concentrated. In Spain I once ate a slice of pumpkin pie that was no more than the bottom half of a medium-sized pumpkin left to cook slowly at the bottom of a stove. The natural sugars on top had caramelised to a sticky blackness, the flesh was as sweet and juicy as I have ever tasted. Aga owners take note.

• Preheat the oven to 200°C/400°F/gas mark 6. Puncture the pumpkin around the top several times with a carving fork, and bake in the oven for 30-40 minutes, until just tender. Remove and cut open with care – there will be quite a lot of steam. When it is cool enough, scoop out the flesh.

• Heat 4 table spoons of olive oil in a large saucepan and gently sauté the onion without colouring for 10 minutes. Add the ground coriander, cumin, turmeric and cayenne pepper and continue to sauté for 2 minutes. The spices should begin to lose their raw aroma and take on a full, rich smell. Add the ginger and garlic and 4 tablespoons of water. Continue to fry until the water evaporates, about 5 minutes.

• Add the pumpkin flesh to the pan, pour over the chicken stock, and season with salt and pepper. Bring to the boil, lower the heat and simmer for 20 minutes. Liquidise in batches, check seasoning and place in preheated thermos flasks.

• To make the relish, roughly chop the red pepper and combine with coriander to taste. Add the sesame seeds and enough olive oil to bind everything together. Serve with the soup.

Saffron, Butter Bean and Ham Hock Soup

SERVES 4

750g/1lb 10oz butter beans, soaked overnight
3 tablespoons olive oil
1 onion, peeled and finely chopped
2 tablespoons finely chopped parsley
1 garlic clove, peeled and finely chopped
1 chilli, deseeded and finely chopped
1 litre/1¾ pints chicken stock
1 cooked ham hock (available from most good butchers)
generous pinch of saffron stamens (or powdered)
salt and pepper

More of a stew than a soup, this is perfect for one of those winter days when a long walk with a picnic has been planned, despite a howling gale fast approaching. Some of my most memorable picnics have taken place, not sitting on a rug beside an idyllic lake in the middle of summer, but huddled in a car, or behind a wall with steaming mugs of soups and great big thick hunks of bread. On such an occasion, the smooth silkiness of the butter beans and that real earthy quality that saffron brings can coax you back to wellbeing. You will need a large-necked thermos, otherwise all the "bits" get stuck at the bottom.

• Cover the beans with plenty of cold water, bring to the boil, remove any scum from the surface, lower the heat and simmer for 30-40 minutes, or until just tender. Drain, reserving the liquid and beans.

• Heat the olive oil in a large pan and sauté the onion without colouring for 10 minutes. Add the parsley, garlic and chilli and continue cooking for 2 minutes, taking care to ensure the garlic does not burn. Return the beans to the pan, along with the stock and the ham hock, bring to the boil, reduce the heat and allow to simmer for 30 minutes.

• Remove the ham hock and gently ease the meat from the bone, chopping it if necessary so the meat is quite well broken up. Return to the pan and discard the bone. Dissolve the saffron in a little of the broth and add to the soup. Check seasoning – the ham hock may be quite salty – and serve or decant into a thermos flask.

Hot Chestnut and Borlotti Bean Soup

SERVES 4

1 onion, peeled and finely chopped
4 tablespoons olive oil
1 bunch of parsley, finely chopped
2 garlic cloves, peeled and finely chopped
1 stick celery, trimmed and finely chopped
2 carrots, peeled and finely chopped
1 sprig of rosemary
1 bay leaf
2 250g/9oz tins borlotti beans, drained
salt and pepper
1 litre/1¾ pints light chicken stock
200g/7oz pack chestnuts

Hot chestnuts and bonfires, dark evenings and chilly days, there is no denying autumn has arrived. Time to move meals indoors? Not in our house. This is just when things start to get interesting. Sausage and mustard sandwiches around a smouldering fire after a morning spent raking up leaves, hot cups of soup all round and tumblers of some fiery red wine. Bonfire night just wouldn't be the same if everything was eaten indoors, the is-it-too-cold debate being half the fun. Warming whisky, then a cup of this soup is a favourite way to start the evening, or ditch the whisky and splash a healthy slurp of sherry into the soup itself, it's time to warm the cockles.

I have a friend who takes a perverse pleasure in shelling chestnuts. Whenever we are away together he likes nothing more than to sit by the fire burning his fingers and, I discovered recently, dipping half the harvest in the sugar bowl before eating it. His claim that 'a lot' of the bag were bad cuts little ice any more. For those who, like me, don't much care for pain, you can now buy vacuum-packed bags of peeled chestnuts.

• Sauté the onion in the olive oil for 10 minutes without colouring. Add the parsley, garlic, celery and carrots and continue cooking for a further 5 minutes. Add the rosemary, bay leaf, borlotti beans, a seasoning of salt and pepper and the stock, bring to the boil, lower the heat and simmer for 45 minutes, adding the chestnuts for the final 20 minutes of cooking.

• Allow to cool, purée half the soup and mix with the other half to serve.

Chilled Cucumber and Yoghurt Soup with Chilli Oil

SERVES 4

1 fresh chilli, deseeded and
    finely chopped
9 tablespoons olive oil
1 onion, peeled and finely
    chopped
1 cucumber, peeled, deseeded
    and roughly chopped
1 bunch of parsley, picked over
    and finely chopped
1 litre/1¾ pints light chicken
    stock
salt and pepper
200ml/7fl oz thick Greek
    yoghurt

Chillies put the fear of God in some people, while in others they generate an almost obsessional enthusiasm – evidence, if it is needed, that they may be addictive. Certainly tolerance is built up. I spent a year travelling in India once and, by the end of it, I invariably garnished my chillies with chillies, although I never got behind the point of vindaloos, a Goan joke lost on me.

You can buy chilli oils, usually in ornate bottles with matching price tag and although they look pretty, I never use enough to finish the bottle before it all starts to taste a bit odd. Added to that, the flavour gets pretty boring. Much more variety is to be had if you combine your chilli and oil each time; that way you can use different chillies and oils. It is also considerably cheaper.

• Combine the chilli with 6 tablespoons of the olive oil and set aside. Sauté the onion in the remaining olive oil for 10 minutes until softened but not coloured. Add the cucumber and parsley, coat well in the oil and pour over the stock. Bring to the boil, season with salt and pepper, lower the heat and simmer for 10 minutes, or until the cucumber is tender. Allow to cool, liquidise to a purée, whisk in the yoghurt and chill.

• Serve with a little of the chilli oil drizzled over.

Chilled Sorrel, Lettuce and Watercress Soup

SERVES 4

2 tablespoons finely chopped
    shallots
2 tablespoons butter
2 tablespoons olive oil
1 garlic clove, peeled and finely
    sliced
150g/5oz sorrel
200g/7oz lettuce (little gem or
    cos)
150g/5oz watercress
6 good size sage leaves
1 litre/1¾ pints light chicken
    stock
salt and pepper
150ml/5fl oz double cream
1 bunch of parsley, chopped

The lemon tartness of the sorrel, silky texture of the lettuce and the peppery fire of the watercress. If you any difficulty finding sorrel, you may find a sprig or two among the herbs in a small, overpriced pack. All the supermarkets say the same thing however; until we buy more, they are unable to supply larger quantities or bring the price down. A chicken and egg argument if ever I heard one. In France you buy it in pillow-sized packs.

One sorrel plant in a pot, provided it is picked often, will grow vigorously all through the summer and usually come back again the next spring.

• Sauté the shallots in the butter and olive oil for 5 minutes without colouring. Add the garlic, sorrel, lettuce and watercress and continue cooking until the leaves wilt. Add the sage and stock, bring to the boil, season with salt and pepper, lower the heat and simmer for 10 minutes. Allow to cool, liquidise, and whisk in the cream. Sprinkle over the parsley and serve.

• Other things to do with sorrel: make into a frittata (see page 26), although you need to cook it into a rough purée first, slice thinly and mix with other salad leaves in a sandwich.

• Other things to do with lettuce: quarter, dress with olive oil, an anchovy fillet or two and some diced roasted red pepper, salt and pepper and a little white wine vinegar; make into a Caesar or salad Niçoise; use for spooning up purées like tabbouleh in place of bread.

• Other things to do with watercress: combine with hardboiled eggs for sandwiches; combine with pears and Manchego cheese and some good olive oil.

Sausages and Mustard

SERVES 4

Mustard and celeriac remoulade

1 small celeriac, peeled and grated into ribbons; 200g/7oz good quality mayonnaise mixed with the same quantity of double cream; 2 tablespoons Dijon mustard; 1 tablespoon capers, well rinsed. Combine the celeriac with the mayonnaise and cream and add the mustard. Coat well and allow to marinate for 1 hour before serving. Garnish with the capers. Spread on the bread, top with a sausage and add more remoulade. Season if necessary. I tend to go for extra mustard.

Mustard and pickles

Choose good-quality pickles, the Japanese and Lebanese both know about pickles and tend to use a less aggressive vinegar. Spread the bread with lots of mustard, slice the pickles and add along with the sausages.

Mostarda di cremona

Italian, and traditionally eaten with boiled meats, Mostarda di cremona goes particularly well with sausages. Fruit is candied whole in a syrup of honey and white wine to which spices and particularly mustard seeds are added. For my money there is rarely enough mustard and in this instance, bright yellow hot English mustard is hard to beat when stirred, streak-like into the syrup.

Beetroot and mustard seed relish

Raw beetroot is best for this, although I have also done it with cooked beetroot. Combine 1 tablespoon of mustard seeds with 3 tablespoons of lemon juice and set aside for at least 30 minutes so the mustard seeds swell. Grate plenty of beetroot on the course setting of your grater. Trim and thinly slice 4 spring onions. Combine the mustard seeds and lemon juice, beetroot and spring onions and bind everything with olive oil. Sandwich, along with the sausages.

These two seem almost wedded to each other, the fire of mustard a necessary foil to the richly meaty sausage. Although that does depend a bit on the sausage. Not for me those neatly wrapped sixes and eights, whether in cling film or greaseproof paper. I want to see my sausages lying loose and naked. Piled in chaos, one speckled sausage intertwined with another, so that when I order the whole is lifted like some living mass. Call me a purist, but for all the flavourings on offer, I tend towards the classic. With names like Directors, or something more straightforward – breakfast, or plain pork when I want a British sausage. I'm not averse to Merguez if it is made well, and Italian pork and fennel can be a delight.

What goes into the sausage is important. Meat needs to be in the majority, very much so. Other 'things' – and I like to know what they are – should be strictly minimal. I'm not too interested in mint for example, preferring to add it, freshly chopped as a dressing if it seems like the right thing to do. What follows are a few favourite ways with sausages although perhaps the best of all is wrapped, still hot in foil, to be eaten not long after cooking with my own pot of English mustard. Dip and eat, dip and eat, dip and eat...

Baguette seems the best bread, its shape as much as anything else its recommendation, but I'm also rather keen on rolling the entire party up in some unleavened Lebanese bread.

Beetroot, Gorgonzola and Horseradish on Rye Bread

MAKES 4 SANDWICHES

200g/7oz cooked beetroot, peeled
8 slices caraway seed rye (if unavailable, use a dark rye with a teaspoon of caraway seeds sprinkled over the filling)
175g/6oz gorgonzola
2 handfuls of salad leaves
1 tablespoon grated horseradish
salt and pepper

It is the Eastern Europeans who know about beetroot. Silky textured, with a sweet, delicate flavour that is so fragile it never lingers for long. Mention beetroot, and everybody invariably starts talking about vinegar. This is to malign the humble beetroot, for it is not its fault that we prefer the industrial pickle to the sweet earthy fresh vegetable. Malt vinegar is fine on something as robust as a good British chip, but not with anything so fine as a beet. Bake your own, or alternatively go for the plainly cooked variety vacuum packed. If you can grow or buy fresh horseradish so much the better, otherwise look out for a jar of horseradish, not horseradish sauce, which is an altogether different proposition.

• Slice the beetroot and cover 4 of the bread slices, allowing a little space at the side for slippage. Beetroot is the last thing you want spilling on to your white linen suit. Spoon the gorgonzola like butter, over the beetroot. Add some salad leaves.

• Sprinkle over the horseradish and a generous seasoning of salt and particularly pepper, top with the remaining bread slices and serve. Beer is a good accompaniment, but go for something from Bavaria or Germany where they know a thing or two about beer making. Alternatively, a British or American microbeer.

Lamb, Minted Crème Fraîche, Avocado and Salted Cucumber Tacos

MAKES 4 TACOS

1 cucumber
salt and pepper
1 bunch of mint, finely chopped
125ml/4fl oz crème fraîche
125g/4oz cold lamb, thinly sliced
1 avocado, sliced
4 tortillas

Tortillas exist throughout Latin America and come in wheat, corn and wheat-corn formats depending on where you are. Tacos is the word used to describe them when they are stuffed, and you can either have tacos soft or hard. Hard simply means they are fried until crisp. My preference is for the soft variety. Perfect for picnics, these large circles of bread can be wrapped around almost anything.

• Peel and deseed the cucumber (to remove seeds, slice in half length ways and cut a V down the full length either side of the seeds, run a teaspoon down through the seeds, which should come away easily). Slice and place in a sieve with a dessertspoon of salt, toss well and set aside for 10 minutes. Rinse under cold water and squeeze gently.

• Combine the mint and crème fraîche and season with lots of pepper. Divide the lamb and avocado between the 4 tortillas, spoon over the crème fraîche and sprinkle on the salted cucumber. Roll up and eat. These tacos will not keep for long. The avocado will discolour and the liquid from the cucumbers and crème fraîche will make the bread go soggy so it is better to make them in situ.

• Alternative stuffings: Hard-boiled eggs, avocado and radish.

• Grated cheese, coriander and smoked chilli salsa – dried smoked chillies, reconstituted in water and mixed with diced tomato, avocado and finely sliced spring onions. To smoke a chilli, dry fry in a hot pan for a few minutes until it smells sweet and smoky.

• Grilled aubergine and red onion with cream cheese and Tabasco sauce.

• Grilled chicken, avocado and crispy bacon with blue cheese yoghurt and chopped shallot.

Pitta Stuffed with Marinated Feta, Tomatoes, Cucumber and Parsley

MAKES 4 SANDWICHES

1 bunch of parsley
200g/7oz feta cheese
1 tablespoon finely chopped shallots
6 black peppercorns, lightly crushed
olive oil
4 small pitta or 2 large ones
4 tomatoes, skinned, cored and deseeded
½ cucumber, peeled and deseeded
salt and pepper

This sandwich has pretty much all the ingredients I associate with the Mediterranean or more specifically Greek holidays. The heat and light so intense it is all you can do to pick away at a salad before collapsing into an armchair in the shade of a midday sleep. The photograph left, was the last shot of the book and two minutes later the sun disappeared over the horizon and we boarded a plane back to London. Pitta bread was destined for sandwiches. Like a good Italian pizza, the bread-to-filling ratio is crucial in any sandwich and a split pitta automatically creates a balance made in heaven. And as if that were not enough, it is sealed in all the right places. None of the bite-and-ooze you get with two slices of open bread, much as I enjoy this kind of sandwich too. With pitta all the juicy bits get pushed up against the sealed edges, golden nuggets at the end of the tunnel.

• Remove the stems from the parsley and roughly chop. Finely chop the leaves and set aside. Combine the chopped parsley stalks with the feta, shallots, peppercorns and enough olive oil to cover. Leave for a few hours, or overnight.

• Lightly dampen the pitta breads and briefly grill until they puff up. Slice the feta, tomatoes and cucumber. Combine in a bowl with the chopped parsley leaves, season with salt and pepper, dress lightly with olive oil and stuff the pittas. If they are travelling, wrap in greaseproof paper.

Grilled Salmon, Roasted Red Peppers and Mayonnaise in Ciabatta

MAKES 4 LARGE SANDWICHES

2 red peppers
olive oil
salt and pepper
500g/1lb salmon fillet, skin removed
2 small ciabatta
1 quantity mayonnaise (see page 157)
4 handfuls frisée lettuce

• Grill the peppers until well charred and set aside in a bowl covered with cling film.

• Lightly oil the salmon, season well with salt and pepper, particularly the salt, and grill until golden and cooked, about 2 minutes each side.

• Set aside to rest and cool.

• Peel and deseed the peppers – if they are still hot, a cold tap helps to save your fingers. Tear into strips.

• Cut the bread in half horizontally. Spread liberally with mayonnaise, divide up the salmon and distribute, place the peppers and then the frisée lettuce on top, finish with the bread and wrap in greaseproof paper.

Terrines and Purées

In France you cannot really picnic without pâté – it would almost be like breaking the law – and it's a habit I have readily adopted whenever I am there. Slices, scoops and large chunks of whatever pâté with lots of bread to accompany. I always try a little bit of everything on offer: 100g of this and 100g of that is better than too much of a bad or indifferent pâté. You get to tell the dry from the moist, the overcooked to the perfect just by looking and it is hard to go too far wrong.

Ingredients for old-fashioned meat pâtés are not the easiest thing to source anymore. Try looking down the meat aisle of your supermarket. Can you find belly of pork, or back fat? A good butcher is more likely to offer successful hunting and will be amenable to mincing to order, provided you give him some warning.

And of course there are all the non-meat pâtés and pastes, dips and purées too. From sweetly simple golden squash to mysteriously smoky aubergine, from the delicate pink of fish roe to the magically dark and glossy olive, these are the purées that take up little room in any picnic basket but supply strong robust flavours required for open-air entertaining.

It is hard to find good shop-bought examples of any of these purées, what tastes fresh and vigorous from your own hand will taste dull and flat from a tub. Too many stabilisers, too few fresh herbs. Even houmous made from tinned chickpeas is far superior to any houmous I have bought ready-made.

A baguette or ciabatta will work well, but for sheer scoopability, try pitta or some of the more pliable Middle Eastern breads now so widely available. Manipulated, origami fashion, into spoons, they too take up little room and seem so well designed for the job. The pleasure to be got from the crustiness of a good French baguette is memorable, but so too is the earthy taste of a dark *pain de campagne*, the bitter-sweet taste of German rye, or the soft creamy texture of an English breakfast bap. *Tortillias* can be delicious, *chapatis* rounded and full-flavoured and I adore Irish soda bread for its simplicity and clean taste.

Real Taramasalata, Pitta, Radish and Olive Salads

SERVES 4-6

50g/2oz stale white bread
125g/4oz smoked cod's roe
juice of 1 lemon
1 dessertspoon finely
    chopped shallot
6 tablespoons light olive oil
2 bunches radishes
125g/4oz green olives

I have been known to eat taramasalata with a spoon, so impatient am I to sample that rich, salty tang of the sea. It is also the texture, like soluble grains of sand – soft and silky. On my first Greek holiday I remember ordering it up in Crete, only to be told that it wasn't available. It was summertime, and this was in the days before seasonality got pushed aside in favour of pleasing the tourists. Ready-made taramasalata has as much to do with the real thing as ready-made houmous and that's not a lot. Gone is all the freshness, the salty tang, the subtle richness. Originally made with the salted roe of grey mullet, smoked cod's roe is more often used now and it gives the dish a delicate and attractive smokiness.

• Remove the crusts from the bread and soak in water.

• Lightly squeeze out the excess water – don't make the bread too dry – and combine with the cod's roe, lemon juice, shallot and olive oil in a food processor. Switch on and blend to a creamy paste. You may need more oil or lemon juice.

• Wash and trim the radishes and sprinkle over a little salt.

• Serve the taramasalata, radishes and olives in separate containers with some warmed pitta bread.

Sardine Pâté

SERVES 4

8 medium-sized fresh
    sardines, cleaned and
    descaled
olive oil
salt and pepper
125g/4oz unsalted butter,
    softened
4 tomatoes, skinned,
    deseeded and roughly
    chopped
1 tablespoon finely chopped
    shallots
2 tablespoons finely chopped
    parsley

If you have made this out of a tin of sardines and think the fresh version will be much the same you are in for a pleasant surprise. This is so much better. A taste of the sea, the richness of the sardines so fresh and vibrant.

• Brush the sardines lightly with olive oil and season with salt and pepper inside and out.

• Grill until cooked and when cool enough to handle remove the flesh from the head and backbone.

• Roughly mash with a fork, incorporating the butter, tomatoes and shallots.

• Stir in the parsley and refrigerate. Serve.

Olive, Garlic and Anchovy Purée with Hard-boiled Eggs

SERVES 4

8 salted anchovy fillets, soaked in several changes of water (or good quality anchovy fillets in oil), roughly chopped
125g/4oz pitted black olives, roughly chopped
1 garlic clove, peeled and finely chopped
125ml/4fl oz olive oil
salt and pepper
juice of 1 lemon
soft or hard-boiled eggs

For such tiny fish, anchovies play a fairly important role in Italian, Spanish, and French cuisine. It is an incredibly meaty flesh for such a sprat. Why are we so hesitant about them? In part it is the quality of the product. Ask anybody about anchovies and invariably they lament their saltiness – how many Caesar salads I have seen eaten sans anchovies, the fish piled, all lonely, at the edge of the plate. Don't grab a tin from the supermarket shelves, go to an Italian delicatessen and if he has them, buy the salted version sold loose from a large white tub. They need soaking in several changes of water, but patience will be rewarded. There is a version of this purée, dark and salty, called tapenade, which comes from Provence and includes capers (from which it gets its name) and often tuna fish (see page 72).

• Place the first 3 ingredients in a pestle and mortar and work into a paste.

• Add the olive oil gradually, as you would for mayonnaise, then season.

• Mix in lemon juice to taste.

At home, this is excellent with soft-boiled eggs. For picnics, I hard-boil the eggs and use this purée in place of salt.

Chickpea and Toasted Sesame Seed Dip

SERVES 4

2 250g/9oz tins chickpeas, rinsed well
2 garlic cloves, crushed to a pulp with a little salt
2 tablespoons tahini*
juice of 2-3 lemons
salt and pepper
1 tablespoon sesame seeds

Soak dried chickpeas if you are catering for large numbers, otherwise the tinned version are a convenient way of buying and not a million miles away from what the Spanish, to name just one country, do. There chickpeas are often sold cooked, off the counter to save the trouble of having to prepare a small quantity at home.

• Puree the chickpeas along with the garlic and tahini, adding a little water until you have a puree the consistency of whipping cream.

• Stir in the lemon juice to taste and season with salt and pepper.

• Lightly brown the the sesame seeds in a dry frying pan and scatter over the purée.

• Chill and serve with lots of bread.

*It makes the task of extracting the tahini from the jar much easier if you sit it in a jug of boiling water five minutes before you need it.

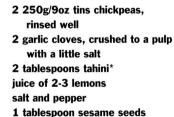

Spiced Butternut Squash Purée with Spring Onion Relish

SERVES 4

1 dessertspoon fresh lime juice and zest of 1 lime
1 teaspoon black mustard seeds
1 onion, peeled and finely sliced
olive oil
1 teaspoon cumin seeds
pinch of cayenne pepper
3cm/1in piece of ginger, peeled and finely chopped
½ teaspoon turmeric
600g/1lb 4oz butternut squash, deseeded, peeled and roughly chopped
salt and pepper
1 bunch coriander, picked over
1 bunch spring onions

Autumn picnics can be some of the most dramatic of the year, when the forecast leaves you undecided about whether a jacket is really necessary for your planned walk through the falling leaves and then a picnic. Butternut squash used to be a rarity but is now widely available. Like most squashes it keeps for ages – in my case often clogging up the vegetable rack for weeks. It has the most delicious nutty flavour with a rich, round, almost voluptuous texture.

• Combine the lime juice and zest with the mustard seeds and set aside.

• Gently sauté the onion in 3 tablespoons of olive oil for 10 minutes without colouring. Add the cumin seeds, cayenne pepper, ginger and turmeric and continue to sauté for a further 2 to 3 minutes, or until the spices lose their raw aroma.

• Add the squash, stirring gently so it is well coated with oil. Pour in 150ml/5fl oz pint of water, bring to the boil, cover, lower the heat and simmer gently for 20 minutes, or until the squash is tender. Allow to cool, liquidise to a purée and season with salt and pepper.

• Roughly chop the coriander and mix in with the purée. Serve with ciabatta and the spring onion relish.

• To make the relish: finely slice the spring onions and mix with the mustard seeds and lime, stirring in a little olive oil to taste, and season with salt and pepper.

Aubergine Purée

SERVES 4

4 large aubergines
olive oil
2 tablespoons finely chopped shallots
1 bunch parsley, finely chopped
1 garlic clove, crushed with a little salt
salt and pepper

The cooking of the aubergine is crucial. Best method of all is slowly over a barbecue so it picks up the smoky flavours essential to the dish's success. Next best is under a grill, and finally in a hot oven. Make sure you prick the aubergines or the flesh is likely to end up bursting or wallpapering your oven.

• Once the aubergines are cool enough to handle, remove the flesh and mash with a fork.

• With a wooden spoon whisk in about 150ml/5fl oz of olive oil much as you would for mayonnaise.

• Stir in the shallots, parsley and garlic, season with salt and pepper, cool and refrigerate before serving.

Broad Bean and Green Olive Purée

SERVES 4

125g/4oz dried skinned broad
   beans, soaked overnight
2 garlic cloves, crushed to a pulp
   with a little salt
2 tablespoons tahini*
juice of 2-3 lemons
salt and pepper
2 tablespoons roughly chopped
   green olives

In the old town of Tripoli in northern Lebanon the narrow market streets buzz with the trading of everything from beans to bomber jackets, silk to soap. Every so often there is a stall selling houmous and fool, the latter a rough textured version of houmous incorporating broad beans. Along with your freshly prepared bowl of each comes some Lebanese bread, a bowl of olives and a bowl of salad, the latter containing large sprigs of the pepperiest mint I have ever eaten, and delicious pickles. Sitting at formica tables eating in the warm October sun, it was a perfect lunch, a real outdoor feast. This purée is a reworked version, to serve with a bowl of fresh salad and large sprigs of mint.

• Cook the broad beans in fresh water until tender – 45 minutes to 1hour.

• Strain, reserving the cooking water and purée along with the garlic and tahini, adding the reserved cooking water until you have a purée the consistency of whipping cream.

• Stir in lemon juice to taste and add the green olives Serve.

*Place the tub of tahini in a jug of boiling water 5 minutes before you need it, which makes it more liquid.

Rough Country Pâté

500g/1lb belly of pork
500g/1lb lean veal
250g/9oz pig's liver
125ml/4fl oz dry white wine
generous splash of brandy
1 garlic clove, peeled and finely
   chopped
1 teaspoon black peppercorns,
   crushed
1 teaspoon juniper berries,
   crushed
pinch ground mace
125g/4oz streaky bacon
salt

This pâté always reminds me of outdoor feasts in France. It is usually too near 12.30 for comfort – I always intend to stop in good time, have a beer while I saunter round choosing a picnic but invariably I try to add just a few more kilometres. The charcuterie is on the edge of closing and the main fear is that the boulangerie will have run out of baguettes. All this edge, however, adds to enjoyment once I have found a field, a running brook in the corner and the dappled light of the sunshine filtered out by rustling poplar trees.

This recipe comes from one of the best books on the subject of French food, Elizabeth David's French Provincial Cooking. *You will probably need to order the meat in advance.*

• Get your butcher to mince the pork, veal and liver together. Combine in a bowl with the wine, brandy, garlic, peppercorns, juniper berries and mace.

• Cut half the streaky bacon into small cubes and add this also, along with a generous teaspoon of salt. Mix, so everything is well coated, cover and leave to stand for an hour or two if possible.

• Pack the mixture into a 1.2-litre/2-pint terrine. Cut the remaining streaky bacon into suitable strips and cover the top of the terrine.

• Preheat the oven to 150°C/300°F/gas mark 2, place the terrine in a bain marie and bake for 1½ hours. Check 20 minutes from the end of cooking, if the pâté is coming away from the sides it is cooked. If you allow it to overcook the inside will become dry.

• Remove from the oven and allow to stand for 30 minutes. Cover with greaseproof paper or foil and weigh down with 2 tins of tomatoes or similar weight overnight in a cool place.

To keep the pâté for longer than a few days, you should obtain pure pork lard, melt it down and cover the surface completely.

Pork Rillettes, Fennel Salad and Caper Berries

SERVES 4

1kg/2lb 4oz belly of pork, trimmed and cut into 1cm/½in strips
200g/7oz back fat, roughly chopped
125ml/4fl oz white wine
3 garlic cloves, peeled and crushed to a paste with a little salt
grating of nutmeg
½ teaspoon ground coriander
3cm/1in cube of ginger, peeled and roughly grated
salt and pepper

4 heads fennel, trimmed
olive oil
lemon juice
125g/4oz caper berries, rinsed and drained (available from good delicatessens)

Silky smooth from Tours or Anjou, slightly more coarse when from Le Mans and La Sarthe, rillettes have a captivating purity. Pork is traditional, along with goose, but also good are rabbit and fish, particularly fatty fish like eel and salmon, sardines and tuna. Meat rillettes will sit quite happily in the fridge for a few days.

• Preheat the oven to 140 C/275 F/gas mark 1.

• Combine the pork and fat, wine, garlic and spices in an oven proof saucepan and season well with salt and very well with pepper. Gently bring to the boil, cover and transfer to the oven for 2 hours, or until the pork is tender.

• Drain into a sieve sitting on top of a bowl. With a knife and fork break up the meat, but don't be too thorough. Remove half the fat from the bowl and add all the meat, toss gently so everything is amalgamated.

• Press lightly into your travelling container and allow to cool. Pour over a covering of extra fat and refrigerate. Leave for a day or two to allow the flavours to develop.

For the fennel salad

• Holding each fennel bulb vertically, cut the thinnest slices possible and place in a bowl, along with 4 tablespoons of olive oil, a seasoning of salt and pepper and a squeeze of lemon juice to taste.

• Add the caper berries to the fennel and serve with the rillettes and some bread. The fennel salad will keep, within its dressing, for a few hours.

Old Fashioned Chicken Liver Pâté with Capers and Cornichons

SERVES 4

200g/7oz butter, softened
piece (or dusting) of mace
piece of cinnamon (about 4cm/1½ long)
225g/8oz chicken livers, trimmed
1 garlic clove, peeled and finely chopped
splash of brandy
1 teaspoon fresh thyme
salt and pepper
generous handful of capers, well rinsed
generous handful of cornichons, rinsed and halved lengthwise
2 tablespoons flat-leaf parsley
olive oil
1 dessertspoon Dijon mustard

Travels well, undemanding on the cook, strong flavour, easy to spread – the essential information on this stalwart of the picnic basket. I have been eating chicken liver pate for as long as I can remember and I still never tire of it. Soft, rich and crying out for red wine, my only problem is when to stop. Just another scoop gets repeated like a mantra.

• Gently melt the butter in a frying pan with the mace and cinnamon to infuse the flavours. Take care not to let the butter get too hot.

• Add the chicken livers and turn the heat up to medium. Toss gently for 5 minutes adding the garlic for the last minute.

• Remove the livers when cooked and place in a liquidiser. Add the brandy to the frying pan away from the heat and stir to amalgamate all the flavours.

• Remove the whole spices and add the liquid to the liquidiser along with the fresh thyme. Season well with salt and pepper, remembering that the pate will be eaten cold, so it needs more seasoning than if it were to be eaten warm, and liquidise. Pack into a suitable container. Allow to cool and refrigerate.

• Combine the capers, cornichons and parsley with 2 tablespoons of olive oil and the mustard, season with salt and pepper and place in a container. Serve with bread.

Pressed Chicken Terrine with Parma Ham, Spinach and Summer Vegetable Salad

SERVES 4

6 corn-fed chicken breasts
500g/1lb large-leaf spinach
salt and pepper
150g/5oz unsalted butter, cut
    into 6 slices
6 slices Parma ham
1 bunch radishes, trimmed
1 avocado, peeled and stoned
½ cucumber, deseeded
1 tablespoon pine nuts
4 tablespoons olive oil
1 teaspoon balsamic vinegar

• Flatten the chicken breasts individually between sheets of greaseproof paper and set aside.

• Blanch the spinach in boiling salted water for 30 seconds, drain and pat dry.

• Layer the spinach over the bottom and sides of a terrine, making sure there is plenty of overlap to cover the top. Place 2 chicken breasts in the bottom, season well with salt and pepper and to with 2 slices of the butter. Lay over 2 slices of the Parma ham and repeat, finishing up with Parma ham.

• Fold over the overlapping spinach. I sometimes add some spinach in the middle layer to give a bit more colour to the finished dish.

• Preheat the oven to 150°C/300°F/gas mark 2.

• Place the terrine in a bain marie and fill with boiling water to come half way up the sides of the terrine. Bake in the oven for 1 hour, or until a skewer inserted into the middle feels hot on your bottom lip – take care.

• Allow to cool for 1 hour and then place 2 or 3 tins of tomatoes or similar on top to weigh it down. When cold, refrigerate for at least 6 hours, or overnight is better.

• Roughly chop the radishes, avocado and cucumber and place in a bowl.

• Fry the pine nuts in a dry frying pan until just coloured on the outside and add to the radishes along with the olive oil, balsamic vinegar and a seasoning of salt and pepper to taste.

• Serve with thick slices of the terrine.

Smoked Salmon, Caper and Green Peppercorn Pâté

SERVES 4

225g/8oz smoked salmon pieces
225g/8oz cream cheese
125ml/4fl oz plain yoghurt
bunch chives, finely sliced
2 teaspoons capers, well rinsed
    and roughly chopped
1 teaspoon green peppercorns,
    well-rinsed
salt and pepper
juice of 1 lemon

Most food shops have good deals located somewhere about their premises. In the case of fishmongers, packets of smoked salmon trimmings are one of the things I go for. Usually deeper in colour than the prime, wafer thin slices already cut, they have all the flavour and succulence and when processed with other ingredients, the colour becomes insignificant anyhow. Grilled ciabatta is a delicious alternative to the more traditional brown bread if you happen to have a barbecue or fire on the go, or split and toasted bagels if you have a good supply of this deliciously chewy bread.

• Combine the smoked salmon, cream cheese and yoghurt and liquidise.

• Stir in the chives, capers and peppercorns.

• Season with salt and pepper and add lemon juice to taste.

• Refrigerate for a few hours before serving.

Tarts, Pies and Pizzas

Tart – as old-fashioned as cooking and yet so fashionable. For all its of-the-moment moderness, however, quirky themes and variations do not sit comfortably within the tart. Grandmother really does know best and the tried and tested combinations are the ones I find work most successfully: apples, pears, spinach, mushrooms, leeks and onions. I don't mind the odd flashy finish here and there; some toasted pine nuts perhaps, or a dribble of truffle oil, but leave the wilder flurries of culinary imagination for indoor experiments. The great outdoors needs the firm hand of experience and a sense of purpose.

A tart is the easiest item to transport, provided you leave it in its tin. This is not a time for delicate pattiserie, delicious as it is, but for something that will take the odd knock or shake and come out triumphant. We are not discussing the finer arts here – perfect circles, straight sides and delicately crimped edges are for home work. The great outdoors demands a more *laissiez faire* approach. Go with the flow.

A general note on pastry

There are as many recipes for shortcrust pastry as cooks and chefs who make it. The one given here is the formula that works for me. If you have your own, then stick with that – I would if the tables were reversed – and if you do try this one I would urge you to use it as a guide. Although the ingredients are simple, as with bread there is enormous variation depending on where you live, water, time of year, air, the flour available and even your mood – hot or cold hands, aggressive or gentle rolling. All of these factors affect your pastry.

Buying pastry

If you are buying ready-made shortcrust, take a look at the list of ingredients on the packet. Some brands, particularly the less expensive ones, make for fairly horrific reading.

A note on utensils

To make a tart you need a tart tin. This is not ceramic, decorated with a picture of some plant or flower, or worse, a recipe, but a thin metal tin with a removable base. Roll the pastry directly on to the

lightly floured base, then lift it into the surround; that way you get to handle the pastry less. Why metal? It conducts the heat more directly and quickly, so your tart bakes, rather than steams. A ceramic flan dish heats up too slowly.

Tartlets make for ease of serving, can be easier to transport and certainly look attractive. You will need to buy individual tins, available from any good kitchen shop.

Shortcrust Pastry

225g/8oz plain flour
pinch of salt
150g/5½ oz butter
1 dessertspoon sugar (a
    generous seasoning of salt
    and pepper for savoury)
1 egg, lightly beaten

* Sift the flour and salt, and then rub the butter in with your fingertips.

* Add the sugar, or salt and pepper, and lightly work in the egg to form a dough.

* Wrap the pastry in cling film and refrigerate for at least 30 minutes, longer if possible.

* Bring back to room temperature and roll out on a lightly floured surface.

Flan dishes come with a removable base. If you roll directly on to this it lessens the handling of the pastry, which is a good thing. Dust the disc with flour and roll out the pastry so it runs over the edge by 2cm/ ¾ in or so. Gently slide a palette knife around the disc and lift into the scalloped edged rim. Lightly but firmly press the pastry into the rim. Chill.

Baking blind – accepted wisdom says you should weigh the pastry down with baking beans. I have never found this necessary; indeed I think it is more inclined to make the pastry steam rather than bake. Preheat the oven to 190°C/375°F/gas mark 5. Prick the base with a fork and bake for 20-30 minutes, until golden brown.

Caramelised Onion and Feta Tart with Baby Spinach and Aïoli Dressing

MAKES 1 26CM/10IN TART

1 quantity shortcrust pastry (see
    above)
olive oil
1kg/2lb 4oz mild onions, peeled
    and sliced
1 tablespoon caster sugar
2 tablespoons finely chopped
    parlsey
1 heaped teaspoon fresh thyme
    leaves
3 garlic cloves, peeled and finely
    chopped
salt and pepper
250g/9oz feta, crumbled
8 generous handfuls baby
    spinach
8 handfuls robust salad leaves
    (eg frisée, little gem)
1 egg yolk
white wine vinegar

Sweet and mild Spanish onions are the ones for this tart if you can get them. I have gilded the lily a bit with spinach and aïoli dressing, but if some remote spot is going to be your dining room you could always dispense with the frills and perhaps even make tartlets which would be easier to transport.

* Roll out the pastry and line the tart tin. Bake the pastry case blind (see above).

* In a large shallow pan, heat 4 tablespoons of olive oil and sauté the onions for 20 minutes, or until soft, turning all the time. Sprinkle over the caster sugar and continue cooking until the sugar caramelises.

* Add the parsley, thyme, 2 of the garlic cloves and a seasoning of salt and pepper.

* Pour the onion mixture into the pastry shell and sprinkle over the feta.

* Bake in a preheated oven, at 180°C/350°F/gas mark 4, for 20 minutes. Allow to cool.

To make the dressing

* Crush the remaining garlic clove with a little salt to form a paste. Whisk in the egg yolk and drizzle in 125ml/4fl oz olive oil, as you would for mayonnaise.

* Thin down with white wine vinegar and warm water to taste and season with salt and pepper.

* Toss with the baby spinach and salad leaves in a bowl and serve with the tart.

As an option, you can marinate feta: slice the cheese and combine with olive oil, black peppercorns and herbs as you wish: parsley, rosemary, thyme. A few crushed cloves of garlic, too, although you need to use it within a day or two or the garlic goes stale.

Mussel and Tomato Tart with Marsh Samphire, Frisée Salad and Toasted Pine Nuts

MAKES 1 26CM/10IN TART

1 quantity shortcrust pastry
(see page 58)
1kg/2lb 4oz mussels
500g/1lb 2oz ripe tomatoes
the leaves from 5 sprigs of
thyme
salt and pepper
2 eggs, lightly beaten
125ml/4fl oz double cream
1 generous handful fresh
marsh samphire
1 head frisée, picked over
and washed
1 tablespoon pine nuts,
toasted in a dry frying pan

As a child I used to pick mussels off the rocks in front of my grandmother's house in County Sligo in the west of Ireland. Curlews would circle, uttering their shrill cry, surely wondering what on earth we were up to. Our harvest of free food came barnacle encrusted and left us with bruised shins as we slipped on the black-granite rocks covered with seaweed. Back to the house where de-bearding would take place in the late afternoon sun, if we were lucky. Often as not, a soft rain would settle, and we would be perched somewhere just inside the door.

These days I pay, like everyone else, for mussels whose beards seem to have disappeared, as have their barnacles. This is all to the good. Provided your mussel is up to scratch. Texture is all in a mussel, texture and a sweet taste of the sea – iodine and brine. Flabbiness is the sign of a bad diet, bad husbandry, or both. Find a good supplier.

• Roll out the pastry and line the tart tin. Blind bake the pastry case (see page 58).

• There are two ways of dealing with the mussels. If they are very fresh and you can spare the time, open as you would an oyster, collecting the juices with the flesh. Alternatively, place in a saucepan, covered, over a moderate heat and steam until just open, no more. About 3 to 4 minutes. Remove the lid and set aside to cool.

• Preheat the oven to 180°C/350°F/gas mark 4. Plunge the tomatoes into boiling water for 10 seconds, remove, allow to cool, take off the skins, remove the core and seeds and slice. Add thyme leaves to taste and season with salt and pepper.

• Add the tomato mixture to the mussels and spread over the tart case. Combine the eggs and cream and pour over the mussels and tomatoes.

• Bake in the oven for 20-30 minutes, or until cooked.

• Trim and wash the samphire, which is the strange tangle of green vegetation shown left, and frisée and combine in a bowl with a dressing made from olive oil, a dash of vinegar and a seasoning of salt and pepper – take care, the samphire is sometimes quite salty – and the pine nuts.

• Toss well and serve with the tart.

Game Pie

**MAKES 1 18CM/7IN PIE WHICH
WILL SERVE 6-8 PEOPLE**

Pastry
550g/1lb 3oz plain flour
150g/5.5oz lard
150ml/5fl oz milk

600g mixed game meat
   (pheasant, partridge, mallard)
300g/10oz pork fat
1 tablespoon Calvados
2 tablespoons chopped parsley
1 teaspoon chopped rosemary
75g/3oz pancetta, chopped
600ml/1 pint game stock
   reduced to 300ml/10fl oz and
   chilled until set

This is a raised game pie, the sort of thing that has fed shooting parties for centuries. For picnics in colder weather it cannot be bettered; full-flavoured and rich with the taste of autumn. Self-contained, the sort of pie that will travel anywhere and still please. Beer, particularly one of the new micro-beers, is a good partner, or some good strong claret. I have a friend who is keen on brandy with this pie, but he has the constitution of an ox. What else to go with it? English mustard works a treat and perhaps some pickles, although choose carefully. Too much malt vinegar will kill the taste and that would be a shame. Chicken and ham make good partners in a raised pie too, but not as good as game. This version is based on a recipe in Good Game by Victoria Jardine-Paterson and Colin McKelvie, one of the better books on the subject.

• Roughly chop the game and combine with the pork fat, Calvados, parsley, rosemary and pancetta. Season with salt and pepper – remember you are going to eat this cold, so don't hold back – and set aside.

• Sift the flour and salt into a bowl. In a saucepan gently heat the lard, milk and 150ml/5fl oz of water until the lard has melted – don't let it boil. Stir this into the flour. Remove a third of the dough and roll the remainder out, as soon as it is cool enough to handle, to line a 18cm/7inch loose-bottomed cake tin, or game pie tin if you have one. Leave the pastry hanging over the edge.

• Place the game mixture in the pastry case, roll out the remaining third of pastry and cover, moistening the edges to seal them. Prick the top to allow the air out and bake in a preheated oven, gas mark 6/200°C for 30 minutes, reduce the heat to gas mark 4/180°C and continue to cook for a further two hours, covering with tin foil if there is any risk of the pastry burning. Leave to cool.

• Gently heat the jellied stock until liquid, make a hole in the top of the pie and pour in. Allow at least an hour for the jelly to set, cut into wedges and serve.

Roquefort, Spinach and Pancetta Tart

MAKES 1 26CM/10IN TART

1 quantity shortcrust pasty (see
    page 58)
1kg/2lb 4oz spinach, well rinsed
75g/3oz pancetta
2 eggs, lightly beaten
150ml/5fl oz double cream
nutmeg
salt and pepper
125g/4oz Roquefort

• Roll out the pastry to line the tart tin. Bake the pastry case blind (see page 58).

• Cook the spinach for the shortest time possible in a large saucepan over a gentle heat stirring constantly – you want it just cooked, so there is a bit of crunch left. Set aside.

• Cut the pancetta into small pieces and fry until crisp in a hot pan. Sprinkle over the pastry and place the spinach on top.

• Combine the eggs and cream and grate over a seasoning of nutmeg, and salt and pepper and pour over the spinach. Sprinkle over the Roquefort and bake until set, about 20 minutes. Serve at room or outdoor temperature.

Other savoury tarts and pies

Mushroom and pigeon; chicken and leek,

Some sweet tarts

Apple, pear and almond are all classics and they work well with an almond paste (equal quantities of butter, sugar, almonds and flour blitzed in a food processor along with an egg to bind it together). Treacle tart for an autumn picnic is a real treat, and lots of cream is vital.

A few other versions

Tarte Tatin is perhaps the most famous, made with apples traditionally, but you can also use pears. Bananas are fashionable, but I'm not so sure. Heat 3 tablespoons of sugar in an ovenproof pan over a moderate heat until caramelised to a dark nut brown, take care not to burn it which can happen quite easily at the end. Spread over the base of the tin. Place peeled and halved fruit in the pan. Top with pastry, puff is traditional, shortcrust also good and bake until the pastry is brown and bubbling. Allow to cool for 5 minutes and upend onto a plate. Whole spices added to the caramel make for a change. Star anise looks particularly pretty.

Old fashioned but suitably rustic is a rough open fruit pie. You can use virtually any fruit for the filling; the principle remains the same – roll out the pastry, place fruit with a little sugar in the middle, fold over the pastry to form an open-topped bag with an 8cm/3¼ in opening and bake in a moderate oven until golden.

Pizza

MAKES 6-8 26CM/10IN PIZZA BASES

450g/1lb strong bread flour
1 teaspoon sugar
15g (3 teaspoons) dried yeast
60ml/2fl oz extra virgin oil

Straight from the wood burning oven, pizzas are hard to beat. Except when, sitting in the middle of nowhere, somebody passes you a piece of warm pizza and you sink back on the grass, glass of beer in hand. It's all in the circumstance.

• Dissolve the sugar in 125ml/5fl oz) warm water, stir in the yeast and leave for 5 minutes in a warm place. It should start to froth up in a gloriously alarming way.

• Add to the flour, along with 100ml/4 fl oz of warm water and the olive oil. Mix to form a dough - you may need more water - and knead for 5 to 10 minutes. Leave to rise for 1 hour or until doubled in size, covered with a damp tea towel. Knock back, split into 6 or 8 balls and roll out thinly.

• Cover with one of the toppings below and bake in the top of the oven, preheated to its hottest setting, for 15 minutes, or until everything is brown and bubbling.

• If serving in the garden, pizza keeps warm for 10 minutes or so. If transporting, wrap loosely in greaseproof paper.

Toppings
Mozzarella, tomatoes and black olives
Bottled artichokes, sliced ricotta and Parmesan
Anchovies, roasted red peppers and rocket
Salami Milano, feta cheese, grilled aubergine and thyme

Leek Pie

SERVES 4

10 medium sized leeks
nutmeg
125g/4oz pancetta, diced
300ml/10fl oz chicken stock
1 egg, beaten
2 tablespoons double cream
1 quantity shortcrust pastry (see page 58)

• Trim the leeks and cut into 3cm/1in lengths.

• Place in a saucepan along with a generous grating of the nutmeg, the pancetta and stock.

• Bring to the boil and simmer, uncovered, for 20 minutes, or until most of the liquid has evaporated.

• Remove from the heat, allow to cool slightly and stir in the egg and cream.

• Transfer to a pie dish and cover with the pastry.

• Bake in a preheated oven, 180°C/350°F/gas mark 4 for 30-40 minutes, or until golden.

• Allow to cool and serve.

Picnic Dishes for Feasts and Parties

Succulent poached salmon, slow baked chicken, steamed vegetables – not all outdoor eating needs to be done on a barbecue. Partial as I am to grilled food, every now and then the chance to cook indoors using a steamer, oven or fish kettle is a welcome change. Healthier too, you might say, but then poached guinea fowl without the aioli is hardly the same, steamed vegetables without lashings of extra virgin olive oil misses the point rather and baked chicken without lots of butter is too worthy by half.

I have always enjoyed cold food, outside particularly, but also for breakfast, there's nothing like a few leftovers to accompany some freshly made coffee.

The meat salads in this chapter are favourites, but any cold meats – ham, salami or left-over roast – tossed with a few vegetables – make excellent dishes. Herbs, particularly parsley, chives, chervil and oregano lift the good to the exceptional and I'm partial to a few pickles. Not, I hasten to add, commercial malt vinegared varieties, which these days are far too acidic. Look instead at ethnic stores; the Japanese are keen on pickles and have retained the skill in making them, Middle Eastern stores, too, are a good hunting ground.

Poached dinners, in the past lamb and beef as well as chicken, are very traditional. The cooking method keeps everything extremely moist and results in the most delicately flavoured stock. Beef and lamb do tend to be a slightly odd colour, but there's the excuse, if one is needed, to whisk up a little mayonnaise, hollandaise or gribiche, salsa verde or tapenade, all to be found in this chapter.

Poaching fish, I was told, was a tricky business and the more I read the more confused I became. Lots of advice on rolling boils, whether it should stay in or out of the water to cool. In my experience, there are two things to pay attention to. Be gentle with fish, it deserves respect and needs to be poached, not boiled to oblivion. Secondly you need to check its state of readiness often, either by pulling gently at the fins, or by examining the flesh close to the bone. As it cooks the fish alters from a raw colour to opaque white. Use the point of a sharp knife and look at the flesh close to the bond. Seafood gets into this chapter because although you can buy it cooked, it really will be much better if you poach it yourself.

For feast do not read formal; this is no time for shirts and ties and evening frocks, just the odd table napkin here and there, a candle or two sitting in jam jars and perhaps a bottle or two of champagne.

Soused Herring, Beetroot and Spring Onion Salad with Crème Fraîche

SERVES 4

8 baby beetroot, or four larger
  ones, baked and peeled
bunch of spring onions, trimmed
  and finely sliced
bunch of parsley, picked and
  finely chopped
1 red chilli, deseeded and finely
  chopped
1 dessertspoon grated
  horseradish
1 tablespoon gherkins, roughly
  chopped
500g/1lb soused mackerel,
  soaked overnight in milk as
  necessary
200g/7oz crème fraîche

Popular in Eastern Europe, herring offer some of the best eating there is. Along with mackerel they used to be popular in this country too, and entire fishing fleets and villages were devoted to these sleek and beautiful fish. I'm no great fisherman, but holidays on the west coast of Ireland usually involved quite a lot of messing about in boats. A line thrown, nonchalantly, out the back invariably produced at least a couple of mackerel and the odd pollack. Smoked in an old biscuit tin on our return, they would be turned into pâté or served as a warm salad.

The sousing of fish is not easy but, where once this process was required as a means of storage, the preservation aspect has become less critical since the advent of refrigeration. Yet commercial producers pile in the vinegar, which can be overpowering and sadly often kicks the fish well into touch. Buy carefully, and soak for a few hours in milk or water to draw out some of the acidity before proceeding.

Baby beetroot can be found in most supermarkets vacuum-packed in fours. If you are lucky enough to find it raw, with leaves attached, snap it up. Beetroot used to be grown not for the root, but for the leaves, which is how it is still sold in Italy. Made into a sauce with tomatoes, onion and garlic, the leaves can make a delicious dressing for pasta.

• Slice the beetroot and arrange on 4 plates. Combine parsley, chilli, horseradish, gherkins, crème fraîche and some salt and pepper.

• Arrange the herring on top of the beetroot and spoon over the crème fraîche and top with spring onions.

• Grate over lots of black pepper and drizzle over olive oil.

Other things to do with fresh herring and mackerel

Japanese and Chinese ingredients like soy and ginger are perfect, cutting the inherent oiliness. Try marinating in a little watered down *teriyaki*. Oatmeal and foaming butter may sound old fashioned but, with a mug of steaming tea, the fish thus crusted and fried make a delicious snack.

Salmon Ceviche, Chive Cream and Lemon Oil

SERVES 4 AS A STARTER

500g/1lb salmon fillet
juice of 3 limes
4 spring onions, peeled and
    finely sliced
dash of Tabasco
2 tablespoons flat-leaved
    parsley, roughly chopped
1 bunch of chives
200g/7oz crème fraîche
salt and pepper
zest and juice of 1 lemon
best quality olive oil

Popular in South America, ceviche is one of the most delicate ways with fish I know. The cure is acid rather than salt, but the principle is the same as with gravadlax: the fish is 'cooked' in that its taste and texture is altered, but it never sees heat. Your fish, consequently, must be of the best quality. Other fish work well, a favourite being cod – I once ate a version in a bar in Barcelona which was divine, and sherry, a chilled fino, undoubtedly, is one of the best things to drink with ceviche.

• Slice the salmon as you would for smoked salmon, as thinly as possible. Combine the lime juice, spring onions, Tabasco and parsley.

• Lay the slices on a shallow plate, making sure they are well coated with the lime juice mixture. Cover with clingfilm and refrigerate for 4 hours.

• Finely chop the chives and add to the crème fraîche with a generous grating of pepper. Combine the lemon zest and juice with olive oil to taste.

• Spread the salmon over plates and serve with a dollop of the chive cream and a generous drizzle of the lemon oil.

• Season with salt and pepper and serve.

Home-cured Gravadlax, Pickled Cucumber and Mustard Sauce

SERVES 10-15, DEPENDING ON THE SIZE OF THE SALMON

200g/7oz salt
200g/7oz sugar
1 bunch of dill, finely chopped
1 small salmon, filleted

1 cucumber, peeled and
    deseeded
1 tablespoon rice vinegar
2 tablespoons Dijon mustard
1 tablespoon crème fraîche
juice of 1 lemon

Traditionally used as one way of preserving fish, fridges mean gravadlax no longer has to serve that purpose. Hold back on the salt, therefore, and let the flavour of the fish shine through. My preference is for a fairly sweet cure with a strong mustard sauce. As for slicing, there is a tendency to go for wafer thin smoked-salmon style slices. For me, fairly thick slices, not quite solid wedges, but not far off.

• Sprinkle the salt, sugar and dill over 1 side of the salmon, place the second half on top and wrap in clingfilm.

• Refrigerate for 24 hours, turning 3 or 4 times. Unwrap and rinse off the cure. Cut in slices.

• Finely slice the cucumber and toss in a sieve with 1 dessertspoon of salt. Leave for 10 minutes, rinse well and pat dry. Combine with the rice vinegar.

• Mix the mustard, crème fraîche and lemon juice to taste. Serve slices of the *gravadlax* with a little of the pickled cucumber and mustard sauce.

Poached Salmon with Tapenade, Broad Bean and Pea Salad

SERVES 6

1 salmon, at least 2kg/4½ lb in weight
1 garlic clove, finely chopped
200g/7oz black olives
6 anchovy fillets (ie 3 anchovies), chopped
2 dessertspoons capers, rinsed in cold water and gently squeezed
juice and zest from 1 lemon
1 bunch of flat-leaf parsley
olive oil
500g/1lb fresh podded peas
500g/1lb podded and peeled broad beans
salt and pepper
1 tablespoon mint, chopped
balsamic vinegar
6 lemon wedges

• Place the salmon in a fish kettle, cover with cold water, add plenty of salt and bring to the boil, simmer for 5 minutes, remove from the heat and leave to cool in the water for 20 minutes. Check to see if it is cooked and either return to the water, or set aside to cool.

To make the *tapenade* combine the garlic, black olives, anchovies, capers, lemon juice and zest and parsley in a blender and blitz briefly to a rough purée with enough olive oil to hold it all together. Check the seasoning and set aside.

To make the salad cook the peas in unsalted water (salted water makes the skins tough). Blanch the broad beans in the same water and remove the skins, return to the water and cook until tender, 2 to 3 minutes. Combine the peas and beans, season with salt and pepper and dress with the mint, a few tablespoons of olive oil and a little balsamic vinegar.

• Arrange the salmon in the middle of a large serving plate, arrange the salad around this and spoon the tapenade along the backbone of the fish. Serve with lemon wedges.

Cajun Bake

SERVES 6

4 small onions, unpeeled
6 chorizo sausages (about 5cm/2in long) each cut into 3
3 medium-sized crabs
1 bunch of parsley
1kg/2lb 4oz prawns
500g/1lb crawfish (optional)
6 limes, halved
plenty of cold beer
1 quantity of mayonnaise (see page 157)
1 quantity of red pepper relish (see page 157)
Tabasco sauce

I've been to some very strange picnics over the years, but one of the oddest, and most fascinating, was west of New Orleans in what the people of Louisiana call the bayou. A group of us boarded an enormous high-powered motor boat and cruised off among the alligators to a 'camp'. This turned out to be a hunter's cabin on stilts in the middle of the swamp lands. As we arrived we could hear cajun music, the band courtesy of our hosts and on the balcony large tables were covered in paper tablecloths. Before we had a chance to sip our ice-cold beers a bucket arrived at the table. Out on to the tablecloth poured our cajun bake, a pile of prawns, crawfish, whole onions, sausages and crabs. Bowls of mayonnaise and tomato relish along with bottles of Tabasco for fire and whole limes completed a feast that went on for several hours.

• Heat a large pan of salted water until boiling. Drop in the onions, chorizo, crabs and parsley, stalks and all. Put the lid on and cook for 10 minutes at a steady simmer.

• Add the prawns, and crawfish if using, and continue cooking for a further 5 minutes.

• Drain, remove the parsley and tip on to a large oval plate, or the table if you wish.

• Decorate with the limes, open the beer and get going. Serve with mayonnaise, red pepper relish and Tabasco sauce.

You may wish to deal with the crabs before everyone starts eating.

• Hold each cooked crab firmly either side of the eyes and bring the back edge down sharply on a firm surface, the underside should now slide away easily.

• Remove the pointed flap along with the 'dead men's fingers' - not be eaten. Crack theclaws, cut the central body in half and start feasting.

Oysters

ALLOW 6 PER PERSON FOR A
FIRST COURSE, 12 FOR A MAIN
(THERE ARE THOSE WHO
CONSIDER 12 A MINIMUM)

To accompany

Tabasco, horseradish, tomato
ketchup, finely chopped shallots
in white wine vinegar, soy sauce
with finely chopped ginger, soy
sauce and wasabi, lemon juice.

What to drink

White wine, although nothing too
delicate, is delicious but I have
to favour Guinness. A dozen with
a pint of the black stuff makes a
perfect lunch.

Alternatives

Angels on horseback, oysters
wrapped in bacon, skewered and
grilled or fried are traditionally
served as a savoury but, I think,
make superb appetisers.

Oysters seem to fall into the love-or-loath school, with passionate eulogising about the merits or otherwise of a native versus Pacific, a number one versus a number three. Personally, I can't see what all the fuss is about. I like oysters, but no more or less than a host of other fish, or meat or vegetables for that matter.

And as for all the fuss over how to eat them, what is wrong with eating them the way you like? In New Orleans I have eaten oysters with horseradish and tomato ketchup, a combination to be recommended. With Tabasco was also popular in the city of Chilli, but so too was lemon juice. Half a dozen served raw on ice before moving on to serious eating is a delight, but try oysters grilled and served with hollandaise, or plopped into a beef and Guinness stew just before serving. Grilled in the shell with a cheese sauce, the more liquid the better, they are hard to beat, and slipped into any fish stew in the final cooking stages, oysters contribute a finesse to be savoured.

Shucking an oyster is not nearly as difficult as it might seem, although it is messy. The skill is in keeping the delicious juice in the bottom half of the shell and not allowing too much of the cracked shell to get into the juices. Time is crucial, as is an oyster knife, a short, blunt, thick-bladed knife and something to protect your hand. Special rubber mats are available, but a well-bunched tea towel does pretty well.

Hold the oyster in your protected hand so the shallow shell is upper-most. Insert the blade of your knife on the right hand side at the back and work it downwards. This is where the muscle holding the oyster closed is located and as you work it loose the shell will open. Remove the shell, place on ice, with seaweed if you have it, and serve.

A knob of garlic butter dropped into an open oyster before flashing it to a melting softness under a preheated grill has to be a favourite way with oysters. Breadcrumbs mixed with parsley and sprinkled on top make this dish even better.

Crab

1 MEDIUM-SIZED CRAB WILL
FEED 2, A LARGE ONE 3-4

To prepare cooked crab, hold the
crab firmly either side of the
eyes and bring the back edge
down sharply on a firm surface,
the underside should now slide
away easily. Remove the pointed
flap along with the dead men's
fingers', which should not be
eaten. The rest is up for grabs,
all the dark meat in the body
section and all the white meat
you can get hold of. Smash the
large claws so diners do not
have to get out their own tool kit
and cut its body part in half;
after that most of the shell is
easily broken with your fingers.

Hold the lobster – of all shellfish it is crab that I crave. Sweet, juicy white meat, a richness which is not overpowering and the full-flavoured dark meat to boot. Travelling back from Cornwall some years ago my last minute shopping before getting on the late afternoon train was a bottle of Mâcon Lugny well chilled and wrapped in newspaper and a whole cooked crab. Along with a few crudities and a tub of homemade mayonnaise, it took 2 hours to eat watching the Cornish coastline slip by and gently removing every last morsel of meat from my crab. I don't know quite what it is about trains and picnics, but they seem so well suited.

Things to eat with crab

Mayonnaise and aïoli (see page 58) probably score most highly on my list; *salsa verde* makes a welcome punchy change; *sauce gribiche*, more usually eaten with *tête de veau* is quite stunning, although my version is not authentic; soy dipping sauce adds a pleasant Eastern touch and pickled ginger supplies the required crunch.

Dressed crab, emptied into an omelette is quite something, particularly when accompanied by some chopped chervil and chives.

Sauce Gribiche

SERVES 2

1 dessertspoon capers, well
    rinsed and roughly chopped
1 bunch of parsley and chervil,
    finely chopped
2 tablespoons mayonnaise
olive oil
salt and pepper
juice of 1 lemon

In sauce gribiche the raw egg yolk of mayonnaise is replaced by a hard boiled one which makes the sauce curiously unstable and slightly tricky to handle. I make a simple and unauthentic version with a little leftover mayonnaise.

• Stir the capers and herbs into the mayonnaise and add enough olive oil to form a sauce.

• Season with salt and pepper and add lemon juice to taste. Serve.

And why stop at crabs?

Apart from the expense, a seafood platter is one of the most dramatic of dishes to serve outside or inside. In France it is often possible to buy the seafood all cooked, leaving only the onerous task of making the mayonnaise and salad up to the host. However you choose to buy, a platter made up of any selection of the following is visually stunning and a delicious feast. Lobster, mussels, oysters, cockles (not actually a favourite), clams, winkles, crab, prawns, langoustine, crawfish. Pile on to ice, or the outside leaves of plenty of lettuce and pass around bowls of mayonnaise and aïoli.

Whole Fish Baked in Salt

I usually buy dourade in portion sizes, but the man in the corner of the market in La Línea, just outside Gibraltar, had enormous, magnificent specimens weighing in at three and four kilos. We bought one of the larger ones. What did we want him to do with it? Were we cooking it in salt, or grilling it? I had been intending to barbecue it, but the salt idea was the obvious answer, very Spanish.

You can, I'm told, cook anything in salt, even chickens, but certainly any whole fish. The curious thing is that both the scales and the insides are left intact. You need a shallow tray, an earthenware cazuela in Spain, but an ordinary roasting tin will do. Spread liberally with rough salt – it must be rough – place the fish on the salt and pack more salt on top. Depending on the size of fish you will need 2 kg/4½lb or more of salt. The fish must be covered with a mountain of salt with no gaps. The fish is then baked (see below for timings) and the salt becomes rock hard. You crack open the salt crust and serve the fish, which will be deliciously moist, having been cooked in a sealed crust so that nothing escapes.

You do not need particularly spectacular salt. Indeed Tidman's bathing salt (made by the same people as the glorious Maldon's sea salt) is fantastically cheap and perfect for this.

The only complication of this way of cooking fish, is the serving. It all gets quite messy and you have to be careful not to let the cooked flesh of the fish come into prolonged contact with the salt or it will be over salty. Crack the top of the salt with a knife sharpener or similar object and remove the slabs of salt before tackling the fish. Delightful as the tiny fish in the photograph are, they are not really suitable for this kind of treatment. Go instead for the likes of sea bream, bass, salmon and red mullet.

• Cooking times are not as long as you might think because salt is a very efficient heat conductor. Preheat the oven to 220°C/425°F/gas mark 7. Timing is difficult to prejudge – experience is necessary. For a large fish, over 1.5kg/3lb 5oz, I usually allow 35 minutes; for anything less than that, about 25 minutes. The crucial thing is not to clean or scale the fish first.

• Serve with plain potatoes and a classic butter sauce, like hollandaise, or something more gutsy, like a fresh relish of red peppers, tomatoes, olive oil and lemon juice.

Seafood Salad, Lime and Chilli Dressing

SERVES 6-8 AS A STARTER

250g/9oz shell-on prawns,
200g/7oz shelled scallops,
    patted dry with kitchen paper
500g/1lb squid, cleaned and cut
    into 2cm / ¾ in pieces
salt and pepper
500g/1lb shell-on clams, cleaned
1kg/2lb 4oz shell-on mussels,
    cleaned
bunch of parsley, picked over
1 red chilli, deseeded and finely
    chopped
extra virgin olive oil
zest of 2 limes and the juice of 1

Seafood salad, fresh, vibrant and tasting of the sea, dressed with best olive oil and lots of black pepper, is a dish I never tire of. Fat juicy prawns, scallops that quiver, squid as sweet as candy and cuttlefish to add weight. Mussels for colour, clams for sweetness, there really is no end to what to put in. Freshness is all, which is why the bought version rarely scores highly. Great if you have a delicatessen that makes it fresh every day, but few of us do. Try instead preparing it at home, using the best of what is available. This photograph was taken in Spain, where the clams are spectacular. Alas there were no scallops available and I wasn't about to serve you, dear reader, with frozen ones.

• Preheat a grill or ridged griddle pan.

• Season the prawns, scallops and squid with salt and pepper and grill until just done, about 2 minutes each side, transferring to a shallow bowl.

• Put the clams and mussels in a saucepan, cover and cook over a medium heat until they open, about 5 minutes. Discard any shells that have not opened in that time.

• Remove some of the excess half shells, they will only be discarded anyway, and add to the prawns, scallops and squid.

• When all the fish is cooked, add the parsley to the bowl along with the chilli, lots of olive oil and the lime zest and juice.

• Season, toss gently and serve.

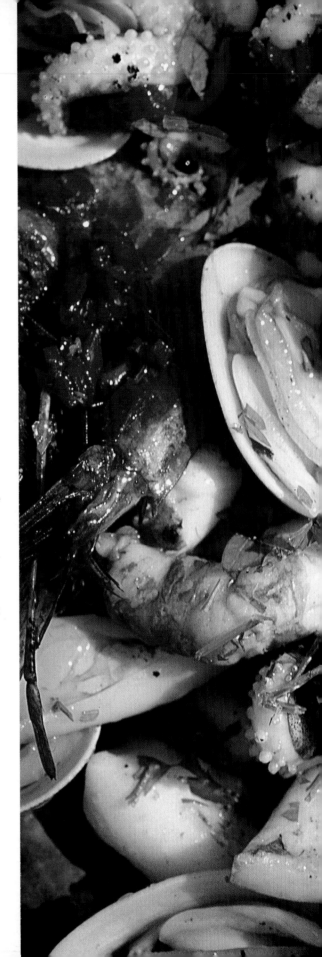

Chicken and Basil Mayonnaise with Spinach and Oven-roasted Tomatoes

SERVES 6

large bunch of basil (or 2 small ones), picked over
1 quantity of mayonnaise (see page 157)
the meat from 1 cooked chicken
salt and pepper
6 handfuls baby spinach
18 halves oven roasted tomatoes (see right)

Oven roasting tomatoes couldn't be easier, particularly if you have an Aga, although a hostess trolley or sufficiently heavy duty plate warmer are also, I'm told, suitable. You need low heat. Sprinkle the cut sides of halved tomatoes with salt and pepper. Drizzle over olive oil and bake for 6 hours or until soft and chewy. A few slices of garlic on each tomato are also delicious.

• Finely chop about a quarter of the basil and roughly chop the remainder.

• Combine all the basil with the mayonnaise and add the chicken, which should be broken into pieces but resist any urge to make them too small.

• Season with salt and pepper.

• Pile the chicken mayonnaise in the middle of plates, surround with the spinach and the halved tomatoes. Serve.

Moroccan-spiced Quail with Pitta, Yoghurt and Coriander

SERVES 4

1 teaspoon cumin seeds
pinch of saffron
½ teaspoon ground cinnamon
3cm/1in piece of ginger, peeled and grated
1 teaspoon paprika
4 tablespoons vegetable oil
salt and pepper
8 quail
2 tablespoons shallots
250ml/9fl oz plain yoghurt
1 bunch of coriander, roughly chopped
4 large or 8 small pitta

You can barbecue or grill these quail and eat them hot, or bake them to eat cold later. I have a passion for cold spiced food, the spices seem more rounded and mellow, the marriage more integrated but there again, picking these quail hot from the grill covered in delicious spiced oil and meaty juices is not something to pass up.

• Lightly toast the cumin seeds in a dry frying pan and grind in a pestle and mortar along with the saffron and cinnamon.

• Combine with the ginger, paprika, vegetable oil and a seasoning of salt and pepper in a bowl.

• With a pair of heavy duty scissors cut down either side of each bird's backbone. Press the quail flat and insert a skewer through its legs to keep it in position. Discard the backbones.

• Place in the bowl along with the shallots and spice mixture, toss well, cover and set aside for as long as possible or overnight in the fridge.

• Grill the quail until cooked – they will take 15 to 20 minutes.

• Combine the yoghurt and coriander and season with salt and pepper.

• Lightly dampen the pitta bread and briefly grill on both sides. Halve the large ones (or leave small ones whole) and serve with the quail along with a well-dressed green salad.

Cold Beef, Salsa Verde and Chicory

SERVES 4

1 large bunch of parsley, finely chopped
1 large of bunch mint, finely chopped
1 tablespoon capers, well rinsed and roughly chopped
1 tablespoon gherkins, chopped
1 garlic clove, peeled and finely chopped
1 desertspoon Dijon mustard
dash of Tabasco sauce
olive oil
salt and pepper
4 heads of chicory, broken into spears
175g/6oz cold rare beef, 200g/7oz if you are feeding enthusiastic carnivores, sliced as thinly as possible

Cold rare beef, sliced thinly, so it melts in the mouth is silky smooth and so delicate. Served with something chilli hot – mustard is a first thought, but even a dash of Tabasco is good – is one of the best ways with beef. The roast the night before may well have been spectacular, but leftovers of this sublime meat make a superb cold plate.

• To make the *salsa verde:* combine the parsley, mint, capers, gherkins, garlic, mustard and Tabasco. Whisk in enough oil to form a thick sauce and season with salt and pepper.

• Arrange the chicory on 4 plates, scatter the beef over and top with the *salsa verde*. More olive oil drizzled over is a good idea.

Other things to do with cold beef

Horseradish is the classic partner. Grate the root directly onto bread spread with crème fraîche, heave in the beef – no point in skimping – season well and eat.

Tossed with soy sauce, a little grated ginger and bean sprouts, sliced beef slides into halved pitta bread for a great sandwich. *Wasabi*, if you like the heat of horseradish, is a good addition but, be warned, it ain't half hot.

Poached Tongue Gremolada, Salad of Radicchio and Peas

SERVES 4

1 salted ox tongue
1 onion, coarsely chopped
1 carrot, coarsely chopped
2 sticks celery, coarsely chopped
1 teaspoon peppercorns
1 bunch of parsley
grated zest from 2 lemons
2 garlic cloves, finely chopped
olive oil
salt and pepper
1 head of radicchio
200g/7oz fresh cooked peas

Picnics were an integral part of summers growing up in Ireland and, along with my mother's pâté, a recipe now sadly lost, the cold cuts that emerged from the basket always included tongue. I adore its melt-in-the-mouth sweetness, rather voluptuous texture and full flavour. To be honest, it's a bit of a trial to cook at home – all that simmering – but the cost saving is enormous. If, however, I'm catering for small numbers, I'm usually to be found queuing up at the deli, along with everyone else. Gremolada is more usually served with ossobuco, but this heady mixture of parsley, lemon rind and garlic goes well with lots of other dishes, not least this poached tongue recipe.

• Rinse the tongue well in plenty of cold water and place in a saucepan. Cover with cold water and bring to the boil.

• Remove the scum and simmer for 10 minutes. Drain, rinse and cover again with fresh cold water. Add the onion, carrot, celery, peppercorns and the stems from the parsley.

• Bring back to the boil, lower the heat and simmer for 4 hours, or until cooked. Stick a skewer into the middle of the tongue and it should meet no resistance at all.

• Leave the tongue to sit in the water for 15 minutes, remove and curl into a tight-fitting round cake tin.

• Put a plate on top and weigh down with about 3kg/6-7lb of weight and leave overnight.

• Finely chop the parsley and mix with the lemon zest and chopped garlic.

• Break the radicchio into leaves, mix with the peas and drizzle over a little olive oil, salt and pepper. Slice the tongue and serve on top with a generous sprinkling of gremolada.

Poached Guinea Fowl, Summer Vegetable and Black Olive Salad with Aïoli

SERVES 4

2 large leeks, trimmed
  and chopped
2 large carrots, trimmed
  and chopped
1 guinea fowl
8 peppercorns
1 bunch of parsley
salt and pepper

500g/1lb French beans,
  trimmed
4 small leeks, trimmed
8 small carrots, trimmed
125g/4oz black olives,
  stoned

2 egg yolks (at room
  temperature)
1 teaspoon good white
  wine vinegar
pinch of English mustard
2 garlic cloves, peeled,
  chopped and mashed
  to a pulp with a little
  salt
300ml/10fl oz vegetable
  oil or light olive oil

* Place the large leeks and carrots in a saucepan, along with the guinea fowl, breast down, peppercorns and stalks from the parsley.

* Season with salt, cover with water and bring to the boil. Remove any scum from the surface, lower the heat and simmer for 1 hour, or until the guinea fowl is cooked.

* Blanch the beans, small leeks and carrots separately in boiling salted water until cooked, remove and refresh under cold water. Set aside.

* Roughly chop the olives. Finely chop the parsley leaves. Set aside.

* Remove the guinea fowl – reserving the stock for later use or freezing – and allow to cool. The flesh will stay more moist if carving is left to the last minute. You may wish for convenience, however, to carve it and wrap in foil.

* Place the egg yolks in a bowl along with the vinegar, mustard, garlic and a seasoning of pepper.

* Beat well and add the oil, drop by drop initially, advancing to a slow but steady stream, whisking all the time, until you have used up all the oil.

* Season with salt and pepper.

* Toss the vegetables with the black olives and parsley and a little olive oil and serve with the guinea fowl and a generous spoonful of the aïoli.

To save split mayonnaise and aïoli

If it looks like its going to split, add a few drops of hot water and you can continue as before. If the aïoli splits right at the end, place 3 tablespoons of hot water in a clean bowl and add the split aïoli as you would for oil to egg yolks.

Duck Salad with Coriander and Mango Salsa

SERVES 4

1 2kg/4½ lb duck
500g/1lb dried noodles
1 dessertspoon sesame
  seeds
4 spring onions, thinly
  sliced
4 tablespoons soy sauce
3 tablespoons vegetable
  oil or light olive oil
½ garlic clove, peeled
  and finely chopped
1 bunch of coriander,
  roughly chopped
1 mango, peeled and
  roughly chopped
125g/4oz pickled ginger

Buy your duck from a good supplier, a good bird tastes sweet and juicy, a poor one tastes of nothing.

* Preheat the oven to 180°C/350°F/gas mark 4. Season the duck well, particularly with salt, and roast for 40 minutes or until cooked, basting with its juices every 10 minutes. Remove the duck and allow to cool.

* Carve the meat from the carcass and shred into bite-sized pieces.

* Cook the noodles as instructed on the packet, drain, refresh in cold water and drain again.

* Toast the sesame seeds in a hot dry frying pan until lightly coloured. Combine with the noodles, spring onions, soy sauce, oil, garlic, coriander, mango and pickled ginger.

* Toss with the duck and serve with extra soy sauce if required.

Baked Spiced Chicken with Lentil Salad and Roasted Garlics

SERVES 4

1 3cm/1in piece of ginger, finely chopped
1 dessertspoon ground cumin
1 dessertspoon ground coriander
1 dessertspoon paprika
1 dessertspoon turmeric
2 lemons
1 medium-sized chicken
1 head of garlic, broken into cloves but left unpeeled
125g/4oz lentils (Puy if possible)
1 bunch of parsley, chopped
1 bunch of coriander, chopped
1 bunch of chives, chopped
salt and pepper

• Combine the first 5 ingredients and whisk in the juice from the lemons. Smear this mixture all over the chicken, working it well in under the skin and set aside for a few hours, overnight is even better.

• Preheat the oven to 180°C/350°F/gas mark 4.

• Place the chicken on its side in a roasting tin and scatter the garlic around it.

• Roast for 1 hour or until cooked, turning the chicken on to its other side after 20 minutes and finally on to its back for the last 20 minutes.

• Remove and allow to rest in a warm place for 15 minutes.

• Meanwhile boil the lentils in plenty of water until cooked, drain and refresh with cold water.

• When the chicken has finished cooking, transfer to a serving plate, along with the garlics. Put the roasting tin back on the heat and stir in the lentils with a little water or stock to scrape up all the residue.

• Stir well so everything is amalgamated and then, away from the heat, add the herbs and a seasoning of salt and pepper.

• Serve with the chicken and garlics.

Lamb Koftas with Quinoa Salad and Raita

MAKES ABOUT 25-30 KOFTAS

500g/1lb minced lamb
2 teaspoons ground cumin
1 chilli, deseeded and finely chopped
1 egg, lightly beaten
salt and pepper
vegetable oil
125ml/4fl oz plain yoghurt
1 dessertspoon finely chopped shallots
1 bunch of coriander, roughly chopped
2 tomatoes, skinned, deseeded and roughly chopped
½ cucumber, skinned, deseeded and finely sliced
100g/3½oz quinoa
1 bunch of parsley, finely chopped
juice and zest of 1 lemon
olive oil

Some of the greatest outdoor feasts I have ever been to were weddings in India. Preparations would go on for days beforehand – marquees, dancers, musicians – and then there was the food. Days in advance the chefs would arrive to prepare the sweetmeats and steadily work their way through the dozens of dishes eventually to be on offer to hundreds of guests. Bride and groom would often arrive on elephants, providing a surreal element to this already spectacular event.

These koftas were often one of the foods set out beforehand, lest anyone was feeling hungry before the main event.

• Combine the lamb, cumin, chilli and egg and season with salt and pepper. Form into balls with a teaspoon and sauté in vegetable oil until brown and cooked.

• To make the raita, combine the yoghurt, shallots, coriander, tomatoes and cucumber. Season with salt and pepper.

• Simmer the quinoa in boiling water for 10-15 minutes, or until just tender. Drain, refresh briefly under running water and mix with the parsley, lemon juice and zest and enough olive oil to keep it moist. Season with salt and pepper.

• Serve the meatballs with the raita on top of the quinoa salad.

Kibbe

MAKES ABOUT 40

For the stuffing
60g/2oz pine nuts
90g/3oz butter
500g/1lb finely chopped onions
200g/7oz minced lamb
2 teaspoons ground cinnamon
2 teaspoons ground allspice
salt and pepper

For the casing
1 onion, peeled and quartered
500g/1lb leg of lamb, boned,
   skinned, defatted and minced
2 teaspoons ground cinnamon
2 teaspoons ground allspice
200g/7oz fine burghul

vegetable oil, for frying

Something of a national dish in Lebanon, where I have feasted on it in one of the most outrageous gardens high in the mountains above Beirut. We sat, reclining on low sofas under awnings stretched from the trees. The sound of water was everywhere and lights and candles were hung from the branches. Kibbe comes both raw – which is how I ate it on that occasion – and cooked. The raw version is a thick purée of the ingredients, delicately seasoned and often including mint or basil. Not everyone's cup of tea, I know, but if you get an opportunity, do try it.

Cooked versions, of which this is one, come in several shapes and forms and, in Lebanese circles certainly, can lead to much discussion and debate on shape, texture and flavour. This version is based on one from Anissa Helou's excellent Lebanese Cuisine *(Grub Street).*

To make the stuffing

• Lightly sauté the pine nuts in the butter until golden brown, remove and allow to drain on absorbent kitchen paper.

• Soften the onion in the butter for 10 minutes without colouring.

• Stir in the meat and cook until it loses all traces of pinkness, mashing and stirring with a fork to prevent lumps forming.

• Remove from the heat and season with the cinnamon, allspice and salt and pepper to taste. Stir in the pine nuts and set aside.

• For the casing, put the chopped onion in a blender and blitz. Add the lamb, cinnamon, allspice and pepper and salt to taste. Blend until smooth.

• Rinse the burghul in several changes of water, drain and add to the meat mixture. With your hands, knead the mixture until you have a smooth paste, about 3 minutes. Divide into about 40 balls.

• Keeping your hands moist to prevent the mixture sticking, mould the burghul mixture in your hand and press with your thumb to make a well in the centre, place about 11/2 teaspoons of the stuffing inside and gently cover by pinching the wrapping around it.

• Place on a tray and continue with the rest. When completed, put the tray in the freezer for 20 minutes to firm the mixture up.

• Heat enough vegetable oil to deep-fry the balls and when sufficiently hot, fry in batches for 3-4 minutes or until golden brown.

• Drain on absorbent kitchen paper and serve.

Barbecues and Fires

Mention barbecues and it is hard not to follow on with thoughts of sizzling steaks, hamburgers and sausages; summer food at its char-grilled best. But why stop there? Vegetables char-grill to perfection, and a whole range of fish like nothing more than some glowing coals to shine on.

And why only barbecues? Bonfires are perfect for baking potatoes, sweet or otherwise, for baking bananas and apples and for grilling steaks. You need the right ironwork, but the heat from bonfire ashes can be just as useful as that from a barbecue; there just isn't quite the same control. The same can be said for your living room fire if you are lucky enough to have one and burn wood. Saturday night? Why not cook steaks over your glowing ashes and then build the fire up again as you settle in front of a great movie.

During the summer I cook on the barbecue most of the time, whether we eat inside or out, but I also use it during the winter – there's nothing quite like a hot barbecued sausage stuffed into bread rolls with lots of mustard after a long walk. In the autumn, too, when afternoons are to be spent trying to clear up the garden, the barbecue comes into its own with the swept-up leaves too damp to sustain a fire of any power.

Most of the following recipes have two parts to them, a salad or salsa and then the actual barbecuing part. When it's raining, switch on the grill.

A note on buying barbecues

You can spend serious money on buying one of the most ancient ways of cooking. Barbecues are easy to make. A few bricks and some old grill trays; a shallow clay flower pot, lined with foil and raised on bricks to allow the air to circulate along with a metal grill tray from your oven; an old biscuit tin, holes punched in the bottom; or for larger numbers, an oil drum cut in half (scrapyards often have cutting equipment). Yet for most of us the convenience of buying the ready-made equipment is too much to resist, so what do you look for?

I started with the cheapest I could find, really to see how much I would use it and how difficult it was to operate. If you are really uncertain, it is probably worth starting with the disposable ones available from petrol stations and hardware stores. They will happily cook a meal for 2 to 4 people, although if you are into large steaks you may need two barbecues, for they are not very big.

The next stage is a charcoal-based barbecue, with a lid if you are considering doing whole chickens or legs of lamb. The cheapest is a sensible way of testing the whole experiment and a portable, charcoal-based barbecue will always be useful to put in the back of the car for picnics.

After that, you start into the serious league and the question of gas has to be considered. If you are feeding large numbers, have hungry children to accommodate and want certainty, consider a gas-fired barbecue. For me, I slip into being primitive man when I barbecue and like the challenge, not that it is particularly great, of charcoal.

It can also be a help, particularly at the beginning, to be able to vary the height of the food from the coals, giving the cook another means of control.

Equipment
Kitchen tongs, both for the charcoal and the food, are essential. Some people like to keep the two separate but I don't bother. After that, most of the equipment sold is either amusing rather than necessary or a duplicate of what you already have in the kitchen.

A note on heat sources
There is a mistaken belief that it is the charcoal that gives barbecued food its unique taste. Not true. You only have to see some of the non-charcoal barbecues to appreciate this. All you need is a sufficient heat source and to be cooking the food a little

distance above it. The charred smokiness in the food occurs as the sugars and fats melt and caramelise on the heat, producing the smoke. It just so happens charcoal is one of the most appropriate heat sources.

When to light, when to cook
Light the barbecue about 15 minutes before you think you should; it only takes a few extra coals to keep it going, and that's far better than facing grumpy hungry faces. About 40 minutes before you intend to cook is the accepted view, and I find is just

about right. Remember that if you are cooking meat it should rest just as it should do when cooked inside. Pushing meat to the cool side of the barbecue when it's cooked will lessen the risk of dry steak.

You don't want the coals too hot, otherwise the food gets too charred. You should be able to hold your hand above the coals for 5 seconds or so before it gets too hot to bear. Don't be afraid to turn things often – you have few controls to hand and turning the food is one of them.

When cooking you want to avoid flames for they can only burn the food. I find one of those plastic plant spray bottles filled with water useful for dampening down any fire. The flames are usually the result of excess fat dripping from the cooking, consequently marinades should be brushed off with some kitchen paper just before cooking.

Lighting
Whether you use lighters or gel, get a small quantity of charcoal going. I use lighters and, using my fingers, pile about 2 handfuls of charcoal on top of the lighter, get that going, then spread it out and pile more charcoal on top.

What type of charcoal to buy
Charcoal is a black, amorphous form of carbon made by heating wood, or other organic matter, in the absence of air. This means the variety of wood is pretty crucial since that is all there is to it. Cheap charcoal is made from cheap wood and 'other' organic matter and neither burns particularly well, or gives off a high enough heat. While it may pay to shop around, it's also worth paying more for your charcoal than the bottom rate for a good brand.

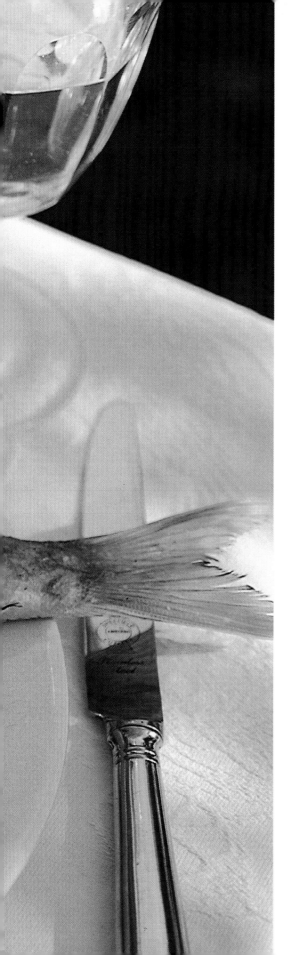

Char-grilled Sea Bream, Courgette Salad and Avocado Salsa

SERVES 4

1 red pepper
4 courgettes
salt and pepper
olive oil
1 bunch of fresh
 oregano

1 ripe avocado
½ bunch of mint
½ bunch of parsley
balsamic vinegar
Tabasco sauce
 (optional)

4 sea bream, each
 about 350g/12oz,
 cleaned but left
 whole with scales
 intact
1 lemon, quartered

Black bream, sea bream, dourade, call them what you will, the delight is in the eating. These are firm-fleshed fish with lots of meat and tough skins, perfect barbecue food. Leave the hollandaise and beurre blanc for something more delicate, this is a fish that responds well to freshly made salsas and relishes, chutneys and pickles, and simply shines on the barbecue. Relatively inexpensive, they often turn up in portion sizes, perfect for the cook who doesn't want to spend an age on a balmy night with a fish slice and candle. Slide on to a plate and serve up straight away. Tell your fishmonger what you are up to so he can leave the scales on. They protect the delicate flesh from the heat, allowing it to cook so it remains moist. Remove the scales, and everything tends to dry out.

• Char-grill the red pepper until blackened all over, wrap in clingfilm and set aside.

• To make the courgette salad, cut the courgettes into strips about 0.5cm/¼in wide and char-grill until just coloured.

• Transfer to a bowl as they are done, seasoning with salt and pepper and tossing with olive oil and a sprig or two of oregano as you go.

• To make the avocado salsa: when the red pepper is cool, peel, deseed and dice it.

• Halve and stone the avocado. To remove the stone, hold the half avocado with the stone in your hand, protected with a tea towel. Bring the knife down sharply on the stone and twist.

• Scoop out and dice (about 0.5cm/¼in squares), discarding the skin.

• Finely chop the mint and parsley. Combine the red pepper, avocado, mint and parsley with 4 or 5 tablespoons of olive oil, a dash of balsamic vinegar and a generous dash of Tabasco, or not, depending on your liking for chilli.

• Cut 2 slashes in each side of each fish, season well inside and out with salt and pepper and barbecue for about 5 minutes each side.

• Serve with the courgette salad, a generous dollop of the avocado salsa and a lemon quarter.

Char-grilled Prawn Kebabs with Soba Noodles and Soy Dipping Sauce

SERVES 4

500g/1lb soba noodles
1 tablespoon finely sliced spring onions
1 dessertspoon pickled ginger, roughly chopped (available in most supermarkets)
1 dessertspoon toasted sesame seeds
1 tablespoon soy sauce
1 chilli, deseeded and finely chopped
1 dessertspoon toasted sesame oil
1 teaspoon white wine vinegar
500g/1lb uncooked prawns with shells still on
satay sticks soaked in water for 20 minutes (this prevents them burning)
vegetable oil and soy sauce, for brushing

My first pleasurable encounter with cold pasta was on a trip to Tokyo. It was Sunday morning and we were on our way to Kamakura, a seaside resort outside the capital. Breakfast was soba noodles eaten with a soy dipping sauce not unlike this one. The noodles are eaten cold, dipped in the sauce. Being the clumsy European I am, I enthusiastically dunked my noodles in the sauce and slurped away – which, I understood, was what you were supposed to do. My hosts started to laugh, not because of my slurping which was quite correct, but because of my dunking. The point, they explained, was to use the soy as a seasoning, not to turf the entire contents of my chopsticks into the bowl. Controlled dipping to about a third of the way in was the tactic they suggested and, sure enough, the flavour of the buckwheat noodles was revealed. I still dislike most cold pasta dishes, but Japanese soba noodles are an exception. To the eagle-eyed among you, the photo is not of soba noodles but of pasta, a perfect substitute.

- Cook the noodles in plenty of salted boiling water as you would any pasta. When they are cooked, drain and plunge into cold water to stop them cooking.

- Drain and place in a bowl along with the spring onions, ginger and sesame seeds.

- Combine the soy sauce with the chilli, sesame oil, wine vinegar and 2 tablespoons of water. Add to the noodles, toss well and check seasoning, you may need more soy. Alternatively, you can keep the soy sauce mixture separate and dip, as for soba noodles.

- Thread the prawns onto the satay sticks or skewers, lightly brush with vegetable oil and soy sauce and grill for 2 minutes each side, or until cooked. Serve on top of the noodles.

Crispy Sea Bass, Spring Greens, Ginger and Coriander

SERVES 4

1kg/2lb 4oz spring greens, trimmed of large stalks and outside leaves
2 carrots, peeled and finely diced
2 celery stalks, finely diced
1 onion, peeled and finely chopped
4 tablespoons olive oil
3 tablespoons soy sauce
1 4cm/1½in piece fresh root ginger, peeled and grated
juice of 1 lemon
4 small sea bass, weighing roughly 350g/12 oz each
1 bunch of coriander, picked over and roughly chopped

- Blanch the spring greens in salted boiling water for 5 minutes, or until wilted, drain and refresh under cold water. In a large saucepan, gently sauté the carrots, celery and onion in the olive oil for 10 minutes without colouring. Return the spring greens and toss so everything is well coated.

- Combine the soy sauce, ginger and lemon juice. Set aside.

- Cut 2 slits in each side of the sea bass (this helps it to cook and prevents it curling up) and season with salt and pepper.

- Barbecue or grill for 4 to 5 minutes on each side, or until the fish is cooked through. With the point of a knife gently ease a little of the flesh away from the bone – if it comes away easily it is done.

- Add the soy mixture to the spring greens, along with the coriander, and toss so everything is heated through. Check seasoning. Serve the fish on top of the spring greens with a little more soy sauce.

SERVES 4
2 tablespoons salted black
beans, well rinsed and
roughly chopped
2 garlic cloves, roughly chopped
1 2cm/³⁄₄in piece ginger, peeled
and finely chopped
½ bunch of spring onions,
trimmed and finely sliced
1 tablespoon dry sherry
2 tablespoons vegetable oil
1 dessertspoon toasted sesame
seed oil
1 dessertspoon sesame seeds
500g/1lb broccoli
4 large herrings (each about
350g/12oz)
2 lemons, quartered

SERVES 4
zest and juice of 2 limes
150g/5oz unsalted butter
4 tablespoons vegetable oil
2 garlic cloves, finely chopped
1 4cm/1½ in piece of ginger,
peeled and finely chopped
6 bok choi, trimmed and rinsed
1 chilli, deseeded and finely
chopped (or to taste)
1 bunch of spring onions,
trimmed and finely sliced
1 tablespoon soy sauce
4 mackerel (each 350g/12oz)
vegetable oil, for brushing

SERVES 4
vegetable oil
2 tablespoons salted black
beans, well rinsed and
roughly chopped
4 garlic cloves, peeled and
roughly chopped
1 4cm/1½ in piece ginger, peeled
and finely chopped
soy sauce
1 tablespoon dry sherry
1 bunch of spring onions,
trimmed and finely sliced
1kg/2lb 4oz squid, cleaned and
trimmed as opposite

Grilled Herring with Broccoli, Black Bean Sauce and Toasted Sesame Seeds

- Combine the black beans, garlic, ginger, spring onions, sherry, vegetable oil and sesame seed oil.

- Toast the sesame seeds in a dry frying pan until lightly coloured and set aside.

- Cook the broccoli in plenty of salted water until tender, drain and toss with the black bean mixture and scatter over the sesame seeds.

- Cut 3 slashes in each side of the herrings and season inside and out with salt and pepper. Brush with a little olive oil and barbecue or grill for 4 minutes on each side, or until cooked.

- Serve with the broccoli and a wedge of lemon.

Char-grilled Mackerel, Bok Choi and Lime Butter

- Combine the lime zest, juice and butter with a seasoning of salt and pepper. Mash together, roll up in clingfilm and place in the fridge.

- Heat the vegetable oil in a wok or large saucepan and, when hot, add the garlic and ginger. Stir and, when golden, add the bok choi and chilli. Carry on stirring and cook for 2 to 3 minutes, or until the bok choi starts to wilt. Add the spring onions, the soy sauce and 1 tablespoon of water. Cook for a further 2 minutes, set aside, cover and keep warm.

- Cut 2 or 3 slits right through to the bone in each side of the mackerel and season the fish well inside and out. Brush with a little vegetable oil and barbecue or grill the fish for 4 minutes each side, or until cooked. Arrange the bok choi on 4 plates, place the fish on top and serve with a slice of lime butter straight from the fridge on each fish.

Char-grilled Squid with Black Bean Salsa

Squid doesn't like being messed about with. Cook it quickly and it's delicious, cook it for a long time and it will be meltingly soft and succulent but anything in between and you are in trouble. Some swear by tenderising squid. Kiwi fruit and mouli are well-known favourites, both contain an enzyme that breaks down the flesh apparently. I'm not so keen, working on the basis that if your squid is fresh and of good quality, there shouldn't be any bother. Frozen squid loses the innate sweetness, which to me is the point of squid.

The beans in this dish are salted black beans available from Chinese stores and increasingly supermarkets. Kidney beans will not do.

- Heat 4 tablespoons of vegetable oil in a wok or large saucepan and when hot, add the black beans, garlic and ginger and stir-fry for 5 minutes over a high heat, making sure it doesn't catch at all. If it looks like drying out, add a few drops of water.

- Add 3 tablespoons of soy sauce and the sherry along with 100ml/3½fl oz of water.

- Stir so everything is amalgamated and simmer for 5 minutes. Add the spring onions.

- Season the squid well and grill for 2 minutes each side. Serve with the black bean salsa.

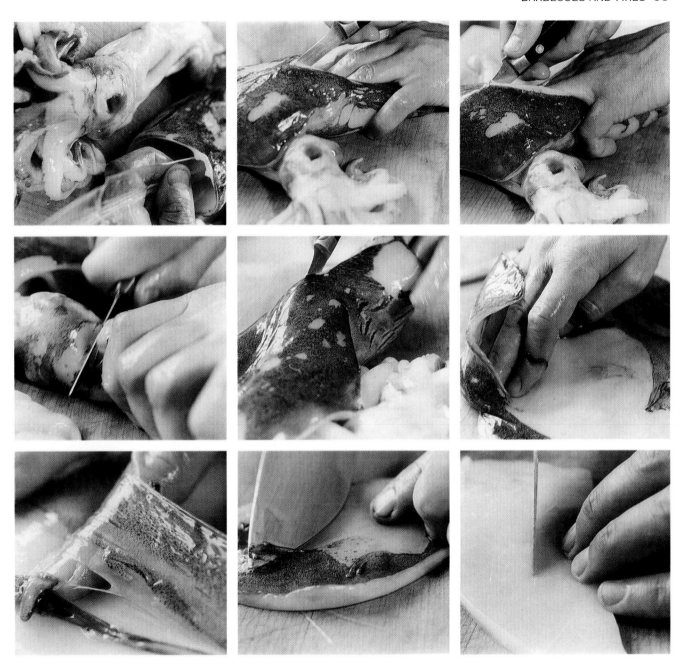

A note on cleaning

As the pictures show, this is rather a messy business, but remarkably simple and satisfying. Most fishmongers will clean squid for you, but rarely the little squid. He is also unlikely to hand over the ink sacks inside, which can be used to dress pasta or as a substitute for cuttlefish ink in risotto nero.

• Slide your finger down the cartilage and pull away from the body sac along with the head.

• Slice off just behind the eyes and discard everything but the tubular body sac, head, tentacles and ink sack .

• Run a knife down the body sac, open out and with your fingers take off the wings. With a knife scrape off the darker-coloured skin and cut into 5cm/2in squares and rectangles. Wash thoroughly and drain.

• With a sharp knife score the outside of the squid in a criss-cross pattern, making sure you don't cut through the flesh. This helps to stop it curling.

Char-grilled Squid with Chilli Oil, Houmous and Rocket Salad

SERVES 4

125g/4oz dried chickpeas, soaked overnight
2 garlic cloves, crushed to a pulp with a little salt
2 tablespoons tahini*
1 bunch of coriander, roughly chopped
juice of 2-3 lemons
2 chillies, deseeded and finely chopped
olive oil
1kg/2lb 4oz squid, prepared as described on previous page
4 handfuls of rocket
1 lemon, quartered

• Cook the chickpeas in fresh boiling water until tender – 45 minutes to 1 hour. They should be nutty, but certainly not al dente.

• Strain, reserving the cooking water, and purée the peas along with the garlic and tahini, adding the reserved cooking water until you have a purée the consistency of whipping cream.

• Stir in the coriander and lemon juice to taste and set aside.

• Combine the chilli with 125ml/4fl oz of olive oil, gently heat until just warm and set aside.

• Barbecue the squid for 2 minutes each side and serve with the houmous, rocket dressed with the chilli oil.

* It makes the task of extracting the tahini from the jar much easier if you sit it in a jug of boiling water 5 minutes before you need it.

Grilled Swordfish Steaks with Chermoula

SERVES 4

2 tablespoons cumin seeds
4 garlic cloves, peeled
2 tablespoons paprika
pinch of cayenne pepper or finely chopped chilli
1 bunch of parsley, picked over
1 bunch of coriander, picked over
4 tablespoons white wine vinegar
juice of 1 lemon
generous dash of good olive oil
4 swordfish steaks, weighing 175g/6oz each
salt and pepper

• To make the chermoula, heat the cumin seeds in a hot dry frying pan until they just release their aroma and blitz briefly in a liquidiser.

• Add the garlic, paprika, cayenne, parsley, coriander and white wine vinegar.

• Blitz again and then add lemon juice and olive oil to taste.

• Heat the mixture in a small saucepan without boiling, and set aside to cool.

• Brush the swordfish lightly with olive oil and season with salt and pepper.

• Grill for 2 to 3 minutes on each side and serve with the chermoula and a few, plainly boiled potatoes.

Chermoula can also be used as a rich and robust marinade for fish before it is cooked. Choose something firm like monkfish, sole or salmon.

Meat and Chicken Satay

SERVES 4

1 walnut sized piece of tamarind
   pulp
2 garlic cloves, roughly chopped
1 tablespoon finely chopped
   shallots
juice and zest of 1 lime
2 tablespoons soy sauce
3cm/1 in piece of fresh root
   ginger, roughly grated
500g/1lb shoulder of lamb,
   cubed
500g/1lb boneless chicken
   thighs, cut into 3cm/1in
   cubes

For the sauce
3 tablespoons plain unroasted
   peanuts, roughly crushed
1 tablespoon vegetable oil
2 red chillies, deseeded and
   roughly chopped
1 garlic clove, peeled and finely
   chopped
2 tablespoons finely chopped
   shallots
juice and zest of 1 lime
125ml/4fl oz coconut milk

Fancy a snack while travelling through Indonesia? If you ever find yourself in this enviable situation the likely answer is going to be satay on skewers. Carefully char-grilled over an open fire, you can eat as you go, or make more of a meal of it, traditionally with cucumber pickle and square chunks of rice cake. A cold beer and some salad are ideal partners.

You need to soak the skewers in cold water for about 1 hour to prevent them burning. Can't wait for that long? Wrap the exposed ends in a bit of foil, fiddly, but it does the trick.

• Place the tamarind in a small cup of warm water and as the pulp becomes malleable squeeze out as much as you can. Drain through a sieve, squeezing out as much liquid from the solids as possible. Discard the pulp.

• Combine the tamarind liquor with the garlic, shallots, lime juice and zest, soy sauce and ginger.

• Thread the meat on to soaked skewers and brush over the marinade.

• To make the sauce, fry the peanuts in the oil until browned.

• Place the chillies, garlic and shallots in a processor and blitz.

• Add to the peanuts and sauté for 5 minutes, stirring all the time to prevent sticking. Add the lime juice and zest and the coconut milk and stir well so everything is amalgamated.

• Cook the skewers over a moderate heat for 20 minutes, turning frequently and basting with any remaining marinade. Serve with the sauce.

Cajun Chicken Wings, Sweetcorn and Avocado Salsa

SERVES 4

1 400g/14oz tin chopped tomatoes
1 onion, peeled and finely chopped
red chillies to taste
4 garlic cloves, finely chopped
125ml/4fl oz red wine vinegar
1 dessertspoon tomato purée
1 tablespoon golden syrup
2 dessertspoons molasses
½ bottle of robust red wine
golf-ball sized piece of tamarind
1kg/2lb 4oz chicken wings

For the salsa
1 280g/10oz tin sweetcorn kernels
1 avocado, peeled and diced
1 tablespoon finely chopped shallot
bunch of coriander, roughly chopped
bunch of parsley, roughly chopped
zest and juice of 2 limes
4 tablespoons olive oil
Tabasco sauce

Chicken wings are the most overlooked part of this delicious bird. Succulent meat, a good quantity of fat to keep them moist and lots of chewing, the latter aspect particularly enjoyable when eating outside. In New Orleans I ate a version of this dish at 5 o'clock in the morning on a street corner with a beaker of beer – the best picnic breakfast after a night spent indulging in jazz.

• Combine all the ingredients except the chicken in a casserole, bring to the boil, lower the heat and simmer, uncovered, for 1 hour.

• Push through a conical sieve, mix into the chicken to coat all the pieces and set aside for an hour or two.

• Combine the first 7 ingredients of the salsa and season with salt and pepper and Tabasco.

• Barbecue or grill the chicken, brushing often with the sauce, and serve with the sweetcorn and avocado salsa and any leftover sauce.

Marinated Leg of Lamb Steaks with Grilled Fennel

SERVES 4

3 medium sized fennel bulbs
olive oil
4 lamb steaks, 175g/6oz each
2 garlic cloves, roughly chopped
(there is no need to peel
them)
1 teaspoon dried oregano
1 chilli, deseeded and roughly
chopped
juice and zest of 1 lemon
salt and pepper

Easy and quick to cook, these steaks give you all the flavour and succulence of a leg of lamb in a fraction of the time. You can certainly cook a whole leg if you choose, although you will need a barbecue with a lid and the patience of an ox, or the kind of foresight I simply don't possess. These steaks will do me fine and leave me free to get on with the part I really enjoy, and that is the marinating. Garlic, herbs and spices, olive oils and vinegars, wines, sherries, shallots and chillies – it is more often a case of what to leave out, for the sign of a good marinade is restraint. Give something to the meat, but don't drown it. And remember dry marinades – a variety of spices mixed with flour will work with almost any cut of meat.

Why dried herbs I hear you cry, I never use dried herbs. Truth is, as soon as this steak hits the heat, whatever is sticking to the outside will burn, not char like the meat so any of the subtlety of fresh herbs is lost while the flavour of dried herbs lingers on.

• Coat the steaks well in olive oil, the garlic, oregano, chilli, lemon juice and zest and a seasoning of salt. Leave aside in a bowl covered with clingfilm overnight.

• Trim the fennel and place on the chopping board. Cut into 0.5cm/¼in slices. Barbecue or grill until well coloured on both sides, transfer to a bowl covered with clingfilm and sprinkle over olive oil and seasoning. Cover quickly so they steam in their own residual heat.

• Brush off the marinade; anything left on will simply burn. Grill the lamb for 5 minutes on each side, turning once or twice, and serve with the fennel.

Sausages, Lentils and Peas with Green Sauce

SERVES 6

1 onion, peeled and finely
chopped
2 sticks celery, trimmed and
finely chopped
4 tablespoons olive oil
2 garlic cloves, peeled and finely
chopped
2 bunches parsley, finely
chopped (reserve the stalks)
1 teaspoon tomato purée
400g/14oz Puy lentils
1 litre/1¾ pints light chicken stock
1 400g/14oz tin tomatoes
1 bay leaf
300g/10oz fresh peas (or frozen
are perfectly good)
1 bunch mint, finely chopped
1 tablespoon finely chopped
gherkins
1 tablespoon capers, well rinsed
1 dessertspoon Dijon mustard
olive oil
1kg/2lb 4oz sausages

This is fantastic party food, a large casserole of lentils and peas, earthy and sweet at the same time, together with char-grilled sausages and a delicious, punchy green sauce. Salad to follow and you've fed the 5,000, well almost. Go for broke on the sausages. My butcher calls his 'Directors' and they are sensational. You do need a good plain pork sausage – leave the flavoured ones for another time and avoid anything with chilli in it. This dish is spiky enough as it is.

• **To cook the lentils and peas:** sauté the onion and celery in the olive oil in a large casserole for 10 minutes. Add the garlic and half the parsley and continue frying for 2 minutes, add the tomato purée and cook for a further 2 minutes, stirring all the time.

• Add the lentils, coat well in the oil and vegetable mixture and then add the stock, tomatoes, bay leaf and the parsley stalks tied together with string.

• Bring to the boil, lower the heat, cover and simmer for 30 minutes, or until the lentils are tender, but still with some bite. Add the peas, and when they are cooked, remove from the heat and season with salt and pepper. Remove and discard the parsley stalks and bay leaf.

• **To make the green sauce:** combine the remaining parsley, mint, gherkins, capers, mustard and enough olive oil to bind the sauce together. Season well with salt and pepper.

• Grill, barbecue, fry or roast the sausages and serve with the lentils and peas and the green sauce.

Hamburgers

500g/1lb minced steak
1 egg

Served up in every fast-food outlet in the world, the burger has come under sustained and powerful abuse. Pure minced steak, seasoned well with nothing more than salt and pepper and gently formed into a hamburger with a little egg to bind it, well now we are talking seriously good food. Char-grilled to give it a crisp, well cooked exterior with a moist, succulent centre – like so many things, when done well it really is delicious. I have never quite understood why pre-formed burgers sell so well. It takes a few minutes to season and form your own and the same time to cook. Serve with Sweetcorn Salsa.

• Combine the meat and egg, season well with salt and pepper, divide into 4 and gently press into a hamburger shape. Grill for 5-8 minutes each side, depending on how well done you like your meat, and serve with one, or all, of the following toppings (each makes enough for 8-10 hamburgers).

Hamburgers with Cream Cheese and Herbs

100ml/3½fl oz double cream
125g/4oz cream cheese
1 small chilli, deseeded and finely chopped
1 tablespoon each finely chopped parsley, oregano, tarragon, chives and chervil
juice and zest of 1 lime

• Combine all the ingredients, stir well to incorporate and refrigerate until needed

Hamburgers with Blue Cheese

100g/3½oz butter, softened
100g/3½ oz blue cheese
1 garlic clove, peeled and crushed with a little salt
1 tablespoon finely chopped parsley

• Combine all the ingredients, stir well to incorporate and refrigerate until needed

Sweetcorn Salsa

1 200g/7oz tin sweetcorn, drained and rinsed
1 chilli, deseeded and finely chopped
1 red pepper, deseeded and finely chopped
bunch of coriander
bunch of parsley
lemon juice
olive oil

• Combine the first 3 ingredients, add the herbs and lemon juice and enough oil to bring everything together.

Lamb Burgers with Goat's Cheese Stuffing

150g/5½oz goat's cheese
1 garlic clove, finely chopped
pinch of cayenne pepper
zest of 1 lemon
2 tablespoons butter
500g/1lb minced lamb

• Combine the first 5 ingredients and mash together with a fork.

• Season the meat with salt and pepper and form into burgers, make a small indent and push 1 teaspoon of the goat's cheese mixture inside before folding the meat around it.

• Grill or barbecue for 5 minutes each side, or until cooked.

Grilled Entrecôte with Field Mushrooms and Bearnaise Sauce

SERVES 6-8

For the reduction
4 tablespoons white wine vinegar
few sprigs fresh tarragon
1 tablespoon finely chopped shallot
1 teaspoon peppercorns

To make the Bearnaise sauce
3 egg yolks
1 tablespoon reduction
250g/9oz butter
1 tablespoon fresh herbs, eg tarragon, chervil, chopped
Salt & pepper

12cm/4in-piece of entrecôte, weighing about 1.5kg/3lb
garlic
olive oil
8 medium sized field mushrooms

Barbecued steaks are great, but it is also worth buying a cut like entrecôte in a large piece. That way you get the smoky, charred outside and a pink, delicate inside. It is much easier to carve along the short side (see right). I don't go in for frills with my beef; buy well, and let the meat do its job. Bearnaise sauce, classic bistro food is fine if you are barbecuing near the house. If you are on location, I'd stick with mustard.

• Combine all the reduction ingredients in a saucepan and add 4 tablespoons of water.

• Bring to the boil and reduce until you have about 1 tablespoon of liquid left.

• Push through a sieve and set aside.

• For the Bearnaise sauce, combine the egg yolks with the reduction in a bain marie or in a heat-proof bowl over a saucepan of gently boiling water. Add the butter, a lump at a time stirring constantly until it thickens. Remove from the heat, stir in the herbs and check seasoning. It will sit, quite happily, for half an hour or so provided it is warm.

• Rub the entrecôte all over with the garlic and then a few tablespoons of olive oil, season well with salt and pepper and barbecue for 10-15 minutes, turning frequently (10 minutes will give rare, 15 minutes medium and 20 minutes almost, although not quite, well done).

• Brush the mushrooms with olive oil and cook/barbecue, gill side up, at the same time. Serve the entrecôte with the mushrooms and Bearnaise sauce.

Marinated Beef Kebabs, Burghul Wheat Salad and Mustard Dressing

SERVES 4

500g/1lb rump steak, cubed
1 red onion, peeled, quartered and separated
2 red peppers, deseeded and cut into small squares
16 small field mushrooms
2 garlic cloves, peeled and finely chopped
few sprigs thyme
bunch of parsley, leaves and stalks separated
sherry vinegar
200g/7oz burghul wheat
bunch radishes, roughly chopped
1 cucumber, peeled , deseeded and chopped
2 courgettes, finely diced
1 tablespoon Dijon mustard
100ml/3 1/2fl oz crème fraîche

My next door neighbours are Iranian and throughout the summer they invariably eat their evening meal outside on rugs and cushions strewn, seemingly carelessly, around the grass. I can't help but peer over the fence, ostensibly to throw a friendly hello in their direction but, if I'm being honest, it's because I have to see what they are eating. From my distant sighting, this is an approximation of one nightly feast.

• Thread the meat, onion, peppers and mushrooms on to skewers and place in a transportable container.

• Combine the garlic, thyme, parsley stalks, a generous seasoning of pepper, sherry vinegar and enough olive oil to make a dressing.

• Pour this over the kebabs and set aside, turning the kebabs every now and then so they are well coated.

• Simmer the burghul wheat in boiling salted water for 8 minutes, or until just tender.

• Drain, refresh briefly under cold water, drain again thoroughly and combine with the radishes, cucumber, courgettes, enough olive oil to moisten and a seasoning of salt and pepper.

• Mix the mustard and crème fraîche and season with salt and pepper. Grill the kebabs or barbecue for 10 minutes, turning and basting occasionally, then serve with the burghul wheat salad and mustard sauce.

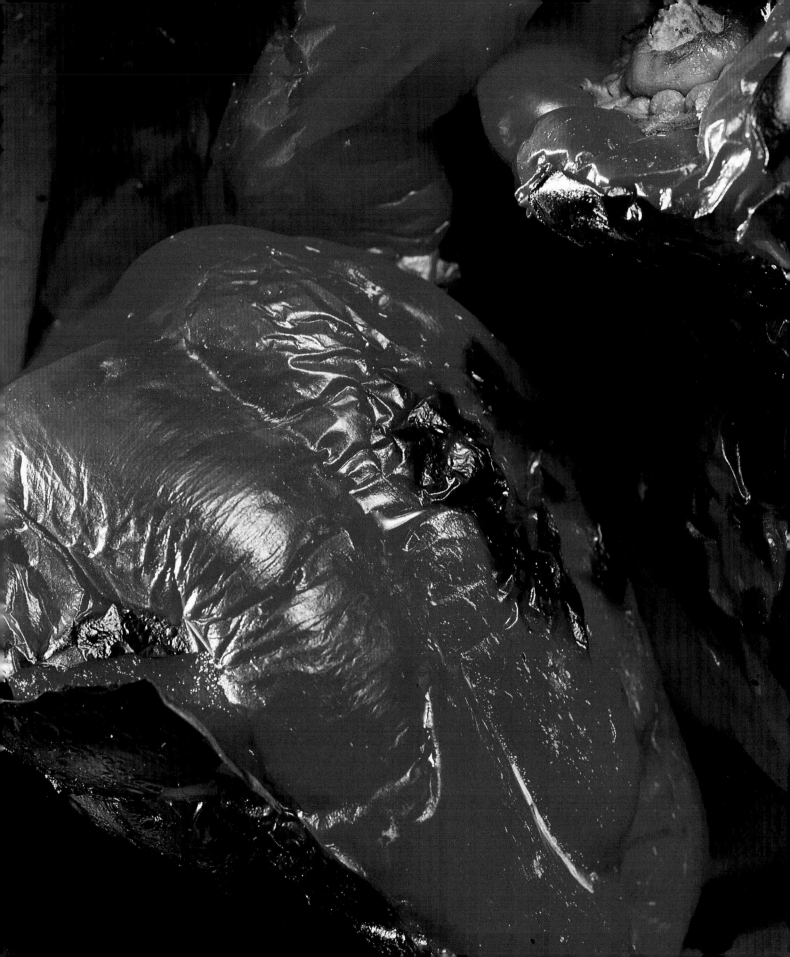

Char-grilled Vegetables

Peppers
Whether you char-grill peppers whole or in strips, the skin needs to be burned black. Once blackened, place in a clean bowl covered with clingfilm so they steam. When cool the skin will slide off. Some people swear by the juices that collect in the bowl but I know lots of chefs who don't bother, rinsing and skinning the peppers under running water. I suspect this is to save their hands and get rid of the seeds.

Other variations
Use balsamic or a good wine or sherry vinegar in place of lemon juice. Garlic, roughly chopped and tossed with the vegetables when they are done is delicious.

Such is my passion for grilled vegetables that I have on occasion tried to grill the most ridiculous things, beetroot and cucumber being notable failures. What is it about that caramelised sticky blackness on the outside of aubergines, peppers and courgettes that is so beguiling, so irresistible? Char-grilled vegetables with couscous, with rice, with mash, by themselves, in a sandwich... I even found myself considering them for breakfast the other morning and was only stopped short by my two-year-old son who simply said 'ugh'.

You can char-grill more vegetables than you might think, although some really need to be cooked before you put them on the grill, perhaps left a little underdone: asparagus, carrots, celery, Jerusalem artichokes, leeks, potatoes and pumpkin fall into this category. Things that might not immediately spring to mind, but which grill well are field mushrooms, red onions, fennel and large beef tomatoes. Undoubtedly the best, however, are red and yellow peppers (leave the green ones out of it, they are bitter and unripe red and yellow ones), aubergines and courgettes.

Some people oil vegetables before grilling them. I would rather add the oil afterwards as the flavour of the oil is preserved, it cuts down on the smoke and tastes better. As far as herbs go, take your pick; basil, oregano and parsley all work well. Remember to season and don't allow the vegetables to char too much, or you won't get to taste the vegetable. Make sure your fire or grill is hot. Grill each vegetable until cooked, transfer to a bowl covered with clingfilm and, as you add each batch, dribble over some olive oil, a little lemon juice and salt and pepper and re-cover with the clingfilm. When you are done, add your chosen herb and toss gently.

Char-grilled Vegetables with Goat's Cheese Crostini

SERVES 4

A selection of grilled vegetables
  (see above)
225g/8oz goat's cheese
12 crostini (see page 22)

- Distribute the vegetables on 4 plates, slice the goat's cheese into discs and lay out on a shallow baking tray.

- Grill until just starting to melt. Transfer to the crostini and serve on top of the vegetables.

- A dribble of some extra virgin olive oil is a welcome addition, or even truffle oil if you have it.

Corn on the Cob

In France they feed maize to animals, in Italy it is milled into polenta and in America it turns up as corn grits and muffins as well as in its natural state. The best corn I have ever eaten was in the markets of India. As I strolled about in the gathering dusk to buy my provisions men sat huddled over tiny barbecues grilling corn; the aroma, mixing with that of the ever present spices, heat and dust, was impossible to resist. A sprinkling of salt and pepper and a generous squeeze of lime – the fruit much sweeter than any I have since had – and my mid-market snack was ready.

• Depending on the degree of charring you like on your corn, you can wrap it in foil (none at all), dampen the husks, having first removed the grassy inner lining (slight char), or remove the husk altogether, soak in water for 10 minutes or so and then turn often (lots of char).

What to dress the cob with?

A favourite remains butter and lots and lots of freshly ground black pepper and sea salt. There must be butter left on the plate so you can roll the husk around in the juices and suck.

Lime and chilli butter

Work a chilli, deseeded and finely chopped, along with the zest of 2 and juice of 1 lime into 125g/4oz softened butter. Chill and use as normal.

Ember-baked Sweet Potatoes, Chilli Butter, Chicken and Tzatziki

SERVES 4

200g/7oz butter, softened
2 chillies, deseeded and
   finely chopped
Salt & pepper
1.5kg/3lb 5oz chicken,
   jointed, or 4 portions
   (legs and thighs are better
   as the breast is inclined to
   dry out)
2 garlic cloves, unpeeled and
   roughly chopped
1 lemon
olive oil
1 tablespoon finely chopped
   shallot
bunch of parsley, stalks
   separated and roughly
   chopped
6 medium sized sweet
   potatoes (the ones with
   the pink skin and orange
   flesh)
large bunch of mint
200ml/7fl oz plain yoghurt

You need the sweet potatoes to be cooked before cooking the chicken so it is as well to put on a few extra, testing is all part of the fun and you can afford to 'lose' a few in the process. Open one up to test and you'll be hard pressed to resist that wonderful sweet steam that rises up to greet you. Put it back in the fire if you must, but why not reach for the butter and indulge in a little tasting while the chicken sizzles away.

• Mash the butter and chilli together, season with salt and pepper, wrap in clingfilm and refrigerate.

• Combine the chicken, garlic, zest and juice of the lemon, a generous slurp of olive oil (about 4 tablespoons), the shallot and the parsley stalks.

• Stir gently so everything is well coated, cover with clingfilm and set aside for a few hours at room temperature, or overnight in the fridge.

• Rinse and dry the sweet potatoes, prick with a fork and wrap in foil. Throw into the embers of your fire and leave for 45 minutes, or until cooked.

• To make the tzatziki: chop the parsley leaves along with the mint leaves and combine with the yoghurt and a seasoning of salt and pepper.

• Wipe the chicken and grill it, turning frequently, until cooked. Serve with the sweet potatoes, chilli butter and tzatziki.

Vegetables
both in and out of salads

Fiery radishes, sweet red onions, or the sharp tangy flavour of a vine-ripened tomato – it's hard to find a vegetable you can really hate. Raw, cooked, even stuffed into supermarket cellophane containers they still look wonderful. Aubergines, courgettes, cauliflowers – even the humble potato has a serenity about it, a wholeness which I find uplifting, almost spiritual. While I am by no means vegetarian, I probably gain more pleasure from cooking vegetables than anything else. Add herbs, olive oil and some lemon juice or vinegar and there is a vast palette to play with.

Not for me the unblemished skins of straight-sided oblong aubergines, the uniform shininess of hot house red peppers. I want my vegetables gnarled and blotchy, sun-streaked and mud-encrusted. I want character and charm together, with a rebellious side to show through. I want my vegetables to look human, to have a breadth and flavour that shows they have lived and enjoyed their sun-baked lives.

Does this mean organic? Not necessarily, but often this is the case. Taste an organic potato alongside the same variety from a mainstream supplier, an organic mushroom or tomato. Is there a contest? I don't believe so. Nor, if you are lucky enough to have your own garden, organic or not, will your own vegetables ever be bettered by the increasingly industrial production of many vegetables.

The demise of our greengrocers is one of the saddest things to have happened on our high street since the Second World War. Although small in number, we have seen the resurgence of butchers, bakers, fishmongers, cheese shops but no comeback of greengrocers. Time for a change.

Stewed, steamed, baked and fried, with olive oil or lashings of delicious butter, with yoghurt or hot mustard dressings these are the vegetable dishes I eat outdoors. Dressings may change, the herb element alter, but they all have full flavours suited to fresh air.

Some Thoughts on a Green Salad

Buy leaves with a variety of colours, textures and flavours. I used to use garlic in the dressing but now rarely do. Mustard only gets in if the leaves are firm and slightly bitter. The olive oil is often single estate, either Italian or Spanish. Salt and pepper are essential and to be used liberally. A splash of water helps to emulsify the dressing.

The acidic element is the main area of contention in a green salad. That and the oil. Some acidic sharpness is crucial, but it plays a supporting role, it should never be prominent. Go easy, you can always add a little more but reversing is out of the question. I use the acid to ring the changes. Lemon and lime juice, rice vinegar for a delicate touch, sherry, red, white wine and so-called balsamic vinegar for something a little robust. Balsamic is a bit of a misnomer, for most of what we get bears little relation to the original. Soy and ginger for an eastern flavour – but then a strong olive oil sits oddly and it's better to go for something neutral like sunflower or groundnut.

You can't mix a green salad until you are ready to eat it. It has no staying power, resilience, or longevity.

Things to add to a green salad: toasted pine nuts, toasted sesame seeds, a dessertspoon of finely chopped shallots, a handful of fresh tarragon or mint, garlic croutons, some crumbled blue cheese, a tablespoon of breadcrumbs sautéed with a little garlic and olive oil.

Little Gem, Blue Cheese Dressing and Garlic Croûtons

SERVES 4

4 thick slices of good white bread
4 garlic cloves, unpeeled and smashed
olive oil
4 little gems, separated
1 tablespoon sherry vinegar
1 tablespoon Dijon mustard
75g/3oz Roquefort, crumbled
Salt & pepper

• Cut the bread into croûton cubes and place on a shallow roasting tray along with the garlic.

• Dribble over a generous quantity of olive oil. Cook under a preheated grill, turning often, until golden brown. Remove and discard the garlic and set the croûtons aside.

• Arrange the little gem leaves in a suitable bowl. Whisk the vinegar into the mustard and then whisk in about 125ml/4fl oz of olive oil.

• Stir in the cheese, mashing it with a fork and season with salt and pepper.

• Pour over the little gems, top with the croûtons and serve.

Potato Salad

SERVES 4

1kg/2lb 4oz potatoes, gently washed
olive oil
balsamic vinegar
1 tablespoon chopped chives

Humble it may be, but the potato is without doubt one of my top vegetables. With a big one bought – piping hot and baked in its skin – from a street vendor in the middle of winter, a park bench picnic suddenly becomes attractive; or sautéed along with a little rosemary and garlic for a mid-week supper in the garden. The range of textures and flavours offered by so many varieties means it is hard to tire of the little – and not so little – tubers. In South America there is a dish called Ajiaco, which includes three different types of potato to provide taste, texture and flavour, and it is astonishing to see how different they all are. Potato salad can be made with mayonnaise, but my own preference is for olive oil.

• Cook the potatoes in plenty of salted water until tender.
Drain and allow to cool slightly.

• Dress, while still warm, with olive oil and 2 teaspoons balsamic vinegar so the potatoes are well coated. Sprinkle over the chives and serve. If you are transporting this salad, don't add the chives until just before serving, or they will wilt.

Old-fashioned Greek Salad

SERVES 4

300g/10oz tomatoes, cored and sliced
1 shallot, peeled and finely sliced
olive oil
salt & pepper
100g/3.5oz black olives
125g/4oz feta cheese, sliced thinly

Old-fashioned because, of late, this peasant dish seems to have attained the status of stardom with 'modern improvements'. I've seen avocados creeping in, along with pine nuts and toasted almonds, roasted peppers and fennel. It is easy to get dictatorial about dishes and it is worth remembering that this is a salad, but in my book the ingredients are established as tomato, onion, salt and pepper and olive oil. After that, the options or extras are limited to cucumber, oregano and possibly green peppers. Feta cheese and olives are also on the list, but nothing else. This is my preferred version, eaten for lunch whenever I am in Greece along with a plate of olive oil-fried chips and a bottle of white wine, although I draw the line at Retsina.

• Arrange the tomatoes on plates or in a shallow bowl. Scatter over the shallot, pour over a liberal quantity of olive oil and season with salt and pepper.

• Add the olives and feta and serve with lots of bread.

Orange, Radish and Rocket Salad with Black Olives

SERVES 4

1 orange
bunch of radishes
4 tablespoons olive oil
dash of red wine vinegar
salt & pepper
4 generous handfuls of rocket
1 dessertspoon chopped shallot
125g/4oz black olives, pitted

Rocket is an outrageous price to buy, particularly when you consider it is not much more than a weed really. Grow your own if you have even the smallest area of soil for an endless supply of pick-and-come-again pepperiness. When the supermarket shelf is my only hope, I mix the rocket with other leaves, including watercress which picks up on the pepper theme.

• With a sharp knife remove the skin and pith from the orange and cut into segments. Trim the radishes and cut into quarters.

• Combine the olive oil, vinegar and 1 tablespoon of water in a salad bowl. Season with salt and pepper and whisk briefly – the water helps to emulsify the dressing.

• Add the orange, radishes, rocket, shallot and black olives to the bowl, toss so everything is well coated with the dressing and serve.

Chicory and Walnuts with Crispy Bacon and Roquefort

SERVES 4

3 tablespoons sunflower oil
    or light olive oil
100g/3½ oz unsmoked
    streaky bacon or pancetta
    cut into lardons
1 tablespoon walnut oil
salt & pepper
juice of 1 lemon
2 heads chicory, trimmed
    and leaves separated
125g/4oz fresh walnuts,
    roughly chopped
200g/7oz Roquefort, lightly
    crumbled

Chicory is a wonderfully versatile vegetable. Gloriously crunchy in salads, it bakes in a moderate oven to a melting softness, but always with that slightly bitter edge. In salads, it refreshes like no other leaf. I rarely bother to wash it, cutting off the outside leaves as necessary and then getting straight on with making it into a salad. It's a good traveller too, being robust enough when left whole to stand up to the odd bump if your picnic is some distance away and you plan to make your salad in situ.

• Heat 1 tablespoon of the sunflower oil in a frying pan and sauté the bacon until crispy then drain on kitchen paper.

• In a bowl combine the remaining sunflower oil with the walnut oil. Season with salt and pepper and add lemon juice to taste.

• Add the chicory and walnuts and toss so everything is well coated. Sprinkle over the Roquefort and bacon and serve.

Panzanella

SERVES 6

4 red peppers
2 yellow peppers
1 large stick French bread
extra virgin olive oil
1kg/2lb 4oz good quality
    tomatoes
4 garlic cloves, peeled, finely
    chopped and crushed with
    a little salt
red wine vinegar
dash of Tabasco sauce
100g/3½ oz capers, well
    rinsed
100g/3½ oz anchovies,
    soaked in plenty of water
100g/3½ oz pitted black
    olives
1 large bunch basil

I eat this salad all the way through the summer, from when the first really tasty tomatoes arrive through to the bitter end. So much do I adore it I wait until I make a disappointing one well into the autumn when the tomatoes are in their final phase. Then it's time to hang up the salad servers, stop buying tomatoes and recognise that colder, wetter weather is on the way. Traditionally made using stale bread, this grilled version is richer and rather more colourful.

• Grill or roast all the peppers until well blackened. Once cool, peel, deseed and slice. Transfer to a bowl and cover with cling film or a damp tea towel.

• Cut the bread into slices, brush with olive oil and grill until just crispy. Place in a bowl.

• Skin, deseed and roughly chop the tomatoes. Do this in a sieve over a bowl so you can save the juice.

• Add the juice and tomato flesh to the bread along with the garlic and peppers. Pour over about 250ml/9fl oz of olive oil and a generous dash of red wine vinegar along with a dash of Tabasco. Stir in the capers, anchovies and black olives.

• Just before serving, tear or cut up the basil leaves, place in the bowl, toss well and serve.

Ratatouille with Crisp Pitta Bread and Cumin-spiced Yoghurt

SERVES 6 AS A MAIN COURSE

3 red peppers
3 onions, peeled and finely
  chopped
6 tablespoons olive oil
500g/1lb aubergines
500g/1lb courgettes
500g/1lb tomatoes
2 garlic cloves, peeled and
  chopped
½ teaspoon coriander seeds,
  roughly crushed
salt & pepper
large bunch of basil, roughly
  chopped
2 teaspoons cumin seeds
150ml/5 fl oz plain yoghurt
6 pitta breads

Ratatouille may seem like one of those stay-at-home dishes – to be served piping hot with a leg of lamb or perhaps some chicken – but I prefer it cold, eaten spoon in hand on the top of a mountain or miles from any road, the oily garlicky juices swimming artistically at the side of a plastic tub. Originally from Provence, this gloriously rich concoction of aubergine, courgette and pepper seems to capture the real essence of summer. Strong colours and flavours and a heady perfume of garlic and herbs.

• Heat the grill and cook the peppers until the skin goes black, transfer to a bowl, cover with clingfilm and set aside.

• Gently sauté the onions in the olive oil for 15 minutes without colouring.

• Cut the aubergines into disks about 1cm/in thick and the courgettes into slightly thinner strips. Lightly brush with olive oil and grill until brown on both sides.

• Drop the tomatoes into boiling water for 30 seconds, refresh under cold water, skin, cut into quarters and deseed. When the peppers are cool enough to handle, remove the skin and the seeds and tear into strips.

• Add the garlic and coriander to the onions, turn the heat up slightly and sauté for 2 minutes. Then add the peppers, tomatoes, courgettes and aubergines, season with salt and pepper and gently stir. Lower the heat and cook for 30 minutes, making sure nothing catches on the bottom.

• Remove from the heat, stir in the basil, adjust the seasoning. Drizzle over the yoghurt and top with the pitta bread. Serve.

• Toast the cumin seeds in a hot dry pan for 2 minutes. Add to the yoghurt, stir well and season.

• Toast or grill the pitta bread until crisp and cut into squares

Aubergine, Spinach and Basil Salad with Garlic Yoghurt Dressing

SERVES 4

2 aubergines, cut into discs
extra virgin olive oil
500g/1lb baby spinach (pre-
  washed packets are ideal)
bunch basil, picked over
2 tablespoons pine nuts
2 garlic cloves, peeled, finely
  chopped and mashed with a
  little salt
3 tablespoons plain yoghurt
1 dessertspoon red wine vinegar

• Brush the aubergine slices lightly with olive oil and grill on both sides until golden brown. When cool, place in a bowl with the spinach and basil. Toast the pine nuts in a dry frying pan until just coloured and add to the bowl along with the garlic, yoghurt, vinegar and 4 or 5 tablespoons of olive oil. Toss everything so it is well coated and serve.

• If you are transporting this salad, hold back on the basil and make the dressing separately, combining everything when you are ready to eat.

Marinated Mushrooms

SERVES 4

125ml/4fl oz olive oil
1 heaped teaspoon caraway
    seeds
generous sprig thyme
black pepper
500g/1lb small field
    mushrooms, wiped clean
    with a damp cloth and
    destemmed
juice of 1 lemon
4 tomatoes, skinned,
    deseeded and cut into
    large chunks

There was a time when mushroom hunting required only an early start as any field used as pasture would sport at least a few in the early morning dew. Fertilisers and chemicals have apparently put paid to all that, but things are changing with Euro-sponsored initiatives like set-aside schemes attempting to reinstate some balance. I doubt we will ever see a complete return, but mushroom hunting has once again become an occasional pastime. Small field mushrooms are what you are after in this dish, take the large ones back for breakfast.

• Combine the olive oil with the same quantity of water in a saucepan large enough to accommodate the mushrooms. Add the caraway seeds, thyme and a generous grind from the pepper mill and bring to the boil. Add the mushrooms, cover and simmer for 10 minutes, or until the mushrooms wilt and become tender. Remove the mushrooms with a slotted spoon and place in a bowl. Boil down the dressing for 5 minutes.

• Add lemon juice to taste, pour over the mushrooms and add the tomatoes, then allow to cool and refrigerate before serving.

• These mushrooms will keep for a day or two in the fridge. Serve with lots of crusty bread and napkins; somehow the oil inevitably ends up dribbling down your chin.

• This same recipe can also be used for courgettes and artichokes, although the latter need to be pre-cooked.

Potato, Cauliflower and Cumin Salad

SERVES 6

200g/7oz potatoes, peeled
1 small cauliflower, broken
    into florets
vegetable oil
1 teaspoon whole cumin
    seeds
1 teaspoon ground cumin
    seeds
1 teaspoon ground coriander
½ teaspoon turmeric
pinch of cayenne pepper
salt & pepper

This salad is actually based on a dry curry of Madhur Jaffrey's to which I am partial not only in the evening, but also for breakfast the next morning. If you can get hold of some good roti it really is a superb feast and easily transportable.

• Cube the potatoes, boil until just tender and drain. Heat 4 tablespoons of vegetable oil in a casserole and, when hot, add the whole cumin seeds and cauliflower.

• Cook for 2 minutes, stirring all the time. Cover, lower the heat and allow the cauliflower to steam in its own moisture for 6 minutes. Add the potatoes, remaining spices and a generous seasoning of salt and pepper. Stir well, so the spices cook in the hot oil. Eat hot, or allow to cool overnight.

Indian tea

This is made by slowly simmering tea, milk, sugar and water together, and is the best accompaniment at breakfast, although a large mug of strong brew is not bad either.

Fresh Japanese Pickled Vegetables

SERVES 4

Vegetables: Leek, carrot, courgette, red pepper, French beans, broccoli stems (the florets tend to get a bit messy), cauliflower, celeriac, celery, cucumber, fennel, turnips.

Marinade
3 tablespoons rice vinegar
3 tablespoons water
4cm/1½ in piece of fresh root ginger, peeled and finely sliced
1 dessertspoon caster sugar

Mention pickles and malt vinegar immediately springs to mind, acidic, flavourless and colourless, its power wiping out any inherent flavour of the ingredient. There are even more ways to pickle than there are vinegars on the market but, where once pickling was essential to preserve, fridges have now made us far less concerned with keeping qualities.

The Lebanese pickle turns a delightful pink, divine with houmous. The French have their gherkins, a joy with pâté, but it is the Japanese who earn supremacy when it comes to pickles. In part to refresh the palate, in part to balance other ingredients, a Japanese meal often incorporates these crunchy vegetables and they work remarkably well in other settings – with pâtés, with fish or even with stews and casseroles.

• Select from any of the vegetables listed and slice as finely as possible – a mandolin is hard to beat for this job.

• Combine with the marinade and refrigerate for 24 hours. The pickles will keep in the fridge for a few days.

Thai-style Chicken Salad

SERVES 4

vegetable oil
2 garlic cloves, peeled and finely chopped
2 dessertspoons Thai red curry paste (available from most supermarkets)
350g/12oz boneless chicken (thigh and leg meat are best) cut into small pieces
50ml/2fl oz fish sauce
pinch of sugar
3 stalks lemon grass, bashed and chopped into 2.5cm /1in lengths
4 lime leaves, finely sliced
200g/7oz medium-sized rice noodles
soy sauce
4 spring onions, trimmed and finely sliced
1 bunch of fresh coriander, picked over and roughly chopped

• Heat 2 tablespoons of vegetable oil in a wok or large saucepan. When hot, sauté the garlic until golden.

• Add the curry paste and chicken and stir so everything is well coated.

• Add the fish sauce, sugar, lemon grass and lime leaves along with 125ml/4fl oz of water and cook, stirring all the time until the chicken is cooked, about 15 minutes.

• Remove from the heat and allow to cool.

• Cook the noodles according to the instructions on the packet, drain, refresh under cold water and drain again.

• Toss with the chicken, 3 tablespoons of soy sauce and the spring onions.

• Remove and discard the lemon grass, stir in the coriander and serve.

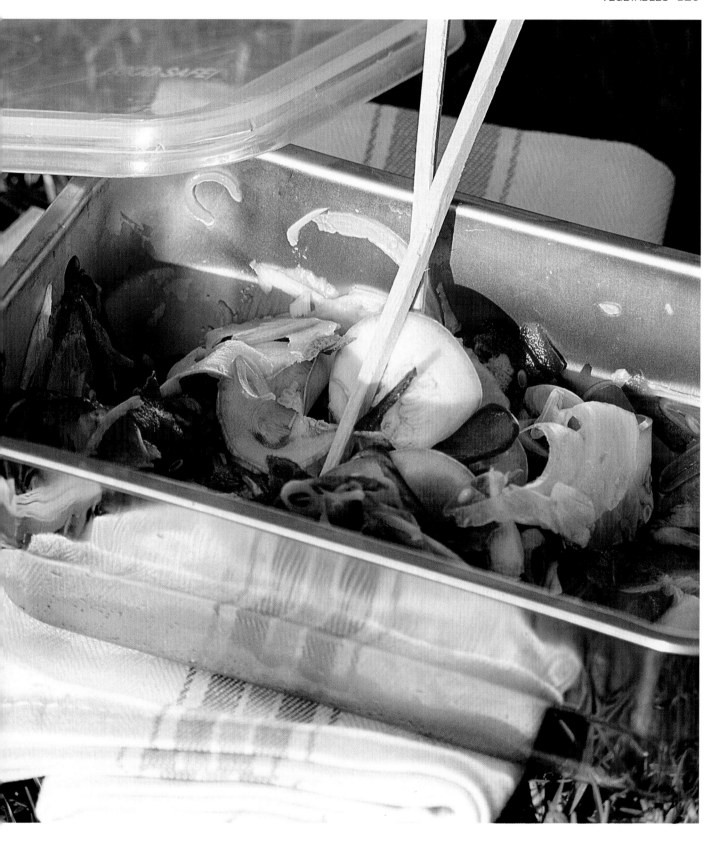

Tabbouleh

SERVES 4

40g/11/2oz burghul wheat
700g/1lb 9oz tomatoes
6 spring onions, finely sliced
2 bunches of flat-leaf parsley,
    finely chopped
1 bunch of mint, finely chopped
generous pinch of ground
    cinnamon and allspice
juice of 1 lemon
extra virgin olive oil
salt & pepper

The key to good tabbouleh is the herbs; the fresher they are, the better the dish, which is maybe why shop-bought is invariably dull and flat. Tabbouleh must be vibrant and alive and if you show the slightest temptation to reach for your food processor, resist. The herbs need to be cut, not bashed into submission. Good tomatoes go without saying. Until travelling in the Middle East I had always been under the impression you used quite a lot of burghul wheat, but there the tendency is to major on the herbs and tomatoes. A much more sensible idea.

• Rinse the burghul thoroughly, drain and place in a bowl. Skin, core, seed and dice the tomatoes. Add them, together with the spring onions, parsley and mint, to the burghul, then mix in the spices, lemon juice to taste, about 125ml/4fl oz of olive oil and a generous seasoning of salt and pepper. Serve with bread and/or with cos lettuce leaves for scooping.

Chickpea and Cherry Tomato Salad with Toasted Pitta and Tahini Dressing

SERVES 4

2 x 400g/14oz tins chickpeas
500g/1lb cherry tomatoes, halved
2 tablespoons chopped shallots
½ teaspoon paprika
pinch of cayenne pepper
1 garlic clove, peeled and finely
    chopped
salt & pepper
juice of 1 lemon
extra virgin olive oil
2 dessertspoons tahini
4 small pitta breads

• Drain and rinse the chickpeas thoroughly. Combine in a bowl with the tomatoes, shallots, paprika and cayenne pepper.

• Mash the garlic with a little salt using the flat side of a large carving knife and add to the chickpeas. Add lemon juice and olive oil to taste and season well with salt and pepper.

• Place the tahini jar in a jug of hot water to soften.

• Combine the tahini with a little hot water and some lemon juice to thin it down.

• Toast the pitta breads and cut into 2cm/¾in squares. Add the pitta to the salad, drizzle over the tahini dressing and serve.

Spiced Aubergine Salad with Ricotta

SERVES 4

2 medium sized aubergines
vegetable oil
1 onion, peeled and roughly
    chopped
4 garlic cloves, peeled and roughly
    chopped
4cm/1½ in piece of fresh root
    ginger, peeled and roughly
    chopped
1 teaspoon turmeric
1 teaspoon ground cumin
1 teaspoon ground coriander
2 teaspoons garam masala
225g/8oz ricotta

• Cut the aubergines into chunks, toss in a bowl with sufficient oil to coat and grill until golden brown and soft.

• Put the onion, garlic and ginger into a blender and purée with 4 tablespoons of water.

• Heat 4 tablespoons of vegetable oil and when hot, add the onion paste. Fry for 5 minutes, or until the paste is lightly coloured.

• Add all the spices and continue to fry for a further 5 minutes, or until the spices lose their raw flavour.

• Add the aubergine along with 125ml/4fl oz of water.

• Stir so everything is well amalgamated and cook for 20 minutes.

• Remove from the heat and allow to go cold. Serve with slices of ricotta on top and lots of bread.

Artichoke and Pea Salad

SERVES 4

300g/10 oz peas (either frozen
    or freshly podded, if the
    latter, you'll need about
    750g/1lb 10oz)
salt & pepper
1 lemon
12 small artichokes or 4 large
    ones
extra virgin olive oil
red wine vinegar
1 bunch parsley, picked over and
    the leaves finely chopped
12 sage leaves (optional)

• Bring a large pan of water to the boil, cook the peas – do not salt the water or it will toughen the pea skin – until just tender, 4 or 5 minutes.

• Remove the peas with a slotted spoon or sieve and refresh under cold water. Salt the water and add the juice and skin of the lemon.

• Trim the stems from the artichokes, cut into quarters or eighths lengthways and add to the water. Simmer until cooked, this should take about 10-15 minutes, depending on the age and size of your artichokes. They are cooked when a leaf pulls away easily.

• Drain the artichokes and place in a shallow bowl with the peas.

• Drizzle over a generous quantity of olive oil, season with salt and pepper and sprinkle over a little vinegar. Scatter over the parsley.

• If using sage leaves, heat a little olive oil in a frying pan and when hot, throw in the sage leaves, they crisp up in a few moments, remove, drain on kitchen paper and scatter over the artichokes. Serve.

Avocado and Chilli Cream with Corn Chips

SERVES 4-6

2 very ripe avocados, halved, stoned and peeled
1 chilli, deseeded and finely chopped
1 dessertspoon finely chopped shallot
4 small tomatoes, skinned, deseeded and finely chopped
1 garlic clove, peeled and mashed to a pulp with a little salt
1 tablespoon finely chopped parsley
1 tablespoon finely chopped mint
juice of 1 lemon
salt & pepper
1 packet of corn chips

Otherwise known as guacamole and a packet of shop-bought corn chips, or how to cheat and get ahead... this is my summer solution to unexpected increases in numbers, a chance to get some breathing space while I try and remember the trick of getting 8 portions out of 1 chicken, or how to obtain an extra 2 servings from the 1 Dover sole I was so looking forward to sharing with my wife. In truth I enjoy the challenge; after all, what is food all about if not sharing it with others, expected or not.

• Combine all the ingredients except the corn chips in a bowl and mash well with a fork. How lumpy or smooth depends on you.

• Season with salt and pepper to taste. Open the packet of corn chips and serve with plenty of cold beers and white wine.

A note on beers:

Until 1997 I was a relatively reluctant beer drinker. A pint on the odd pub occasion and a bottle of something cold and lagerish in the fridge was as far as I went. Far more interesting, I thought, to drink wine.

It was while researching several pieces on beer for a men's magazine that the world of micro beers was revealed. Small, at least initially, in size, the essence of a micro beer is that it is brewed by someone who looks at the whole brewing process with a fresh eye. Britian obviously has a very old brewing tradition but in recent years that tradition has become clouded as the large breweries have taken over. Brewers of micro beers are looking carefully at the hop and malt characteristics and brewing beers with extraordinary depth and character.

Pioneered in America, where the tradition of micro beers is well established, the growth in Britain, Australia and New Zealand is to be welcomed. Added to that is a realisation of the quality of the beer coming from Bavaria, the Czech Republic and Belgium. There are literally hundreds out there, we've every reason to experiment.

Leek Vinaigrette, Herb and Cream Cheese Crostini

SERVES 4

1 bunch parsley
1 bunch thyme
6 sage leaves
225g//8oz cream cheese
salt & papper
1kg/2lb 4oz leeks, trimmed and cut into 2.5cm/1in lengths
extra virgin olive oil
white wine vinegar
12 crostini (see page 20)

• Chop the herbs and mash into the cheese with a fork, season with salt and pepper and set aside.

• Steam the leeks until cooked, transfer to a shallow bowl and pour over 4 tablespoons of olive oil, a generous seasoning of salt and pepper and a splash of vinegar.

• Cover with cling film and set aside.

• To serve, distribute the leeks on 4 plates, spread the cream cheese on top of the crostini and place on top of the leeks.

Eggs, Salt and Spices

Hard-boiled eggs are central to many picnics and outdoor feasts. Straight from the shell, with sea salt; made into egg mayonnaise with plenty of chives and parsley or roughly chopped and sprinkled over any number of salads.

For an elegant touch, try hard-boiling quail eggs. The shells are attractive and their size makes them the perfect mouthful to snack on. What to eat with them? Maldon's sea salt would be my first choice, and after that any number of the following, preferably in neat piles on an elegant plate: celery salt, ginger, freshly roasted and ground cumin seeds, freshly ground black pepper, ground cinnamon.

What hen eggs lack in elegance, they gain in sheer size and this is all to the good when talking about the more chunky accompaniments like chermoula (page 100), tapenade (page 72) and salsa verde (page 82). Also good are flavoured oils, either with herbs or with chilli.

A note on buying eggs:

It is not easy, buying an egg these days. Where once they came from hens, you would be forgiven for thinking they now come from anywhere but a hen – farm fresh, barn fresh, free range, organic free range – these seemingly meaningless titles adorn egg boxes like billboards and serve only to confuse.

I am less concerned about the organicness of an egg than about the husbandry involved. As a result I tend to buy my eggs from a small retailer who has visited the farm and can tell me a bit about it. My egg then seems, on the basis of experience, to have more chance of a viscous white and deep yellow yolk. A happy hen lays a better egg.

Quinoa Salad with Sherry Vinaigrette and Quail's Eggs

225g/8oz quinoa
1 red pepper, deseeded and finely diced
1 bunch radishes, trimmed and finely diced
half cucumber, skinned, deseeded and finely diced
2 sticks celery, trimmed and finely diced
bunch spring onions, finely diced
1 courgette, finely diced
12 quail's eggs
extra virgin olive oil
sherry vinegar
juice of 1 lemon

Bit of a super-food, quinoa, containing complete proteins rather than the incomplete ones associated with most grains. That said, I like eating it more because of its gentle flavour and crunchy texture than because of its protein structure, although vegetarians may be particularly interested in its make up. A new grain? Not quite, the Incas in South America were keen on it and its still grown in Bolivia and Peru. So what can you use it for? It absorbs about double its volume in water or stock so is great for pilafs and risotto-style dishes. Accompaniments? As with most grains, strong flavours like chilli, tomato, garlic and spices.

• Cook the quinoa in plenty of salted water until just tender, about 10 minutes. Drain and mix with the red pepper, radishes, cucumber, celery, spring onions and courgette.

• Hard-boil the quail's eggs, they take about 5 minutes. Combine 5 tablespoons of olive oil with salt and pepper to taste, a teaspoon of sherry vinegar and lemon juice to taste.

• Add this to the quinoa and toss well, you may need more oil or lemon juice. Top with quail eggs and serve.

Roasted Red Pepper, Anchovy and Caper Salad

SERVES 4

6 red peppers
100g/3½oz anchovies, rinsed
1 tablespoon capers, well rinsed
salt & pepper
extra virgin olive oil

You cannot afford to be timid about the roasting of red peppers. Black skins mean black skins and you will achieve the required intensity only if you leave them alone to roast over or under an intense heat. Barbecues, I have found, are easily the best method but a grill or hot oven also work well. Don't be tempted to turn the peppers too often, they need to sweat it out.

Once sufficiently well roasted – and I mean black, really black – transfer to a bowl and cover with clingfilm or a damp tea towel. This way they steam a little in their own heat, which makes lifting the skin easier. When cool enough to handle, remove the skin and deseed. If you are in a hurry you can do this under a running tap – you lose the rather delicious juice, but better that than burning your fingers.

Yellow and green peppers: yellow are also suitable, being the same as red, only a different colour. Green peppers, however, are not suitable, being unripe and bitter.

• Roast the peppers until the skin is well blackened, transfer to a bowl, cover and set aside to cool.

• Remove the skins, deseed and cut into thin strips. Combine in a shallow bowl with the anchovies, capers, salt and pepper to taste and a generous slurp of olive oil.

• Serve with lots of fresh bread.

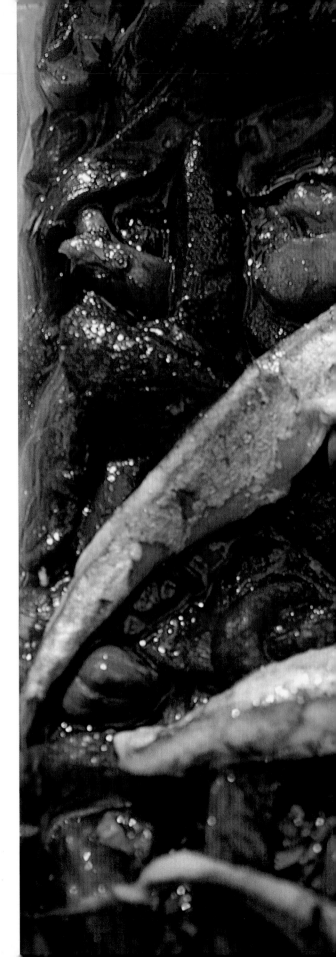

Piperade with Saffron Rice

SERVES 4

6 red peppers
olive oil
2 onions, peeled and sliced
250g/9oz jamon serrano ham, sliced and cut into bite-sized pieces
6 tomatoes, skinned and deseeded
salt & pepper
2 eggs
generous pinch of saffron strands
300g/10oz basmati rice

One of the most stunning drives I have ever done was from the tiny fishing port of San Sebastian on the northern Spanish coast over the Pyrenees and into France. We managed 4 picnics over the 2 days and each one took place at the top of at least 3 valleys. The sun shone and every afternoon after a long and lazy lunch feasting on the local salamis, cheeses and rough-hewn vegetables we would gaze at the ever changing shadows in each of the valleys, the sun slowly sinking out in the Atlantic.

I am a fiend when it comes to tapas and invariably order too many things. This piperade was one casualty of over-ordering, so we asked the man running the bar to wrap it in foil for us. Several hours later, it formed part of a three-valley lunch, as good cold as it was hot. If you are barbecuing and have a suitable earthenware bowl, you can cook the piperade at the side – it goes well with pretty much anything.

Adding saffron early on in the cooking process gives colour to the dish, a deep, almost mysterious yellow that seeps into the dish. Add it later on and you get more of the flavour, that bright earthiness, which is why I've divided it up.

• Roast the peppers until well blackened, transfer to a bowl and cover with clingfilm or a damp cloth. When cool enough to handle, peel, deseed and roughly chop.

• Heat 3 tablespoons of olive oil in a pan and gently sauté the onions for 10 minutes without colouring. Add the ham and continue cooking for 5 minutes, stirring all the time.

• Add the tomatoes and the peppers, season with salt and pepper and cook, constantly stirring, for a further 20 minutes.

• Break the eggs into the hot sauce, stir and cook until just set. Check seasoning and serve.

• Meanwhile, divide the saffron into 2 piles; add half to a pan of salted water, pour in the rice and boil until tender, about 15 minutes.

• Drain and combine with the other pile of saffron, soaked in a little warm water.

• Toss well and serve with the piperade.

Spinach Salad with Bacon and Hot Mustard Dressing

SERVES 4

olive oil
1 dessertspoon Dijon mustard
balsamic vinegar
salt & pepper
Tabasco sauce
125g/4½ oz streaky bacon or pancetta
4 generous handfuls baby spinach
4 generous handfuls of other salad leaves

I'm a sucker for bags of baby spinach. All washed and neatly packaged it beats the endless rinsing associated with this delicate, silky leaf. Tender and juicy, almost sweet, it makes a delicious salad. The more adult leaves can be left to cook with cream and nutmeg another day.

• Whisk 4 tablespoons of olive oil into the mustard in a large salad bowl. Add a teaspoon of balsamic vinegar and salt and pepper to taste.

• Add Tabasco to taste – you may need more olive oil.

• Cut the bacon or pancetta into lardon-sized pieces and sauté in a little olive oil until crispy.

• Add the spinach, salad leaves and bacon to the dressing, toss well and serve.

Haricot, Tomato and Radicchio Salad

SERVES 4

olive oil
1 dessertspoon Dijon mustard
1 garlic clove, peeled, finely chopped and mashed with a little salt
salt & pepper
2 tennis-ball sized heads of radicchio
6 large tomatoes, cored, quartered and deseeded
250g/9oz tin haricot beans, rinsed and well drained
½ bunch mint, chopped
½ bunch basil, chopped

Make this salad before you head into the great outdoors and by the time you sit down everything is deliciously amalgamated, the leaf sufficiently wilted. The man pictured below is selling arbutus unedo, a curious little round prickly red fruit which has very little flavour. It is the symbol of Madrid, is liked by bears, but tends to be used for decoration, hence the necklaces he is making.

• In a large bowl or plastic box whisk 4 or 5 tablespoons of olive oil into the mustard along with the garlic and a seasoning of salt and pepper.

• Core, trim and chop the radicchio. Add to the dressing with the tomatoes and beans and toss to coat in the dressing. Before serving, sprinkle in the herbs and toss well.

Desserts
when a bar of chocolate will not do

A favourite late-summer dessert is a bowl of figs and a large, darkly-forbidding bar of chocolate. If a journey is involved, the figs get wrapped in greaseproof paper to shield them from damage. If a grill is anywhere to hand they are likely to be flashed under it to a caramelised sweetness, as in the recipe on page 146 but whichever way it is, the combination never ceases to be a joy.

As to the remainder of the desserts in this chapter, I have concentrated mostly on fruit. Outdoor eating, for the most part, coincides with the wealth of fresh fruit and these recipes aim to make the most of their already excellent flavour. Cakes like the almond and lemon corn cake along with the truffle cake are delicious served with fresh raspberries or strawberries, but will work equally well with a caramelised orange salad, or a salad of summer fruit.

Syllabub is decadent and old-fashioned, two delicious reasons, if any were needed, to resurrect this ancient English dessert. Variations are endless offering much scope for the cook. So too with fruit fools, rhubarb to plum, peach to melon. Possibly my favourite pudding is not actually something to eat at all, but a slightly chilled glass of Sauternes.

Brown Sugar Meringues, Strawberries and Cream

SERVES 4

100g/3oz egg whites
200g/7oz light soft brown
   unrefined sugar
500g/1lb 2oz strawberries
buckets of whipped cream

Meringues are misunderstood in my view. All that debate about whether the interior should be chewy or not. Where is the debate? A dry meringue is like eating cardboard, only worse, it has no texture, no substance. Give me chewy any day, that gloriously soft toffee-stick-to-the-mouth gooeyness is what I want in my meringue and if I can have flavour, so much the better. There is a current vogue for so called unrefined sugars, by which they really mean less refined. Certainly "unrefined" seems to me to have more substance and is worth seeking out.

• Preheat the oven to 110°C/225°F/gas mark 1.

• Whisk the egg whites in a bowl until stiff. Add 100g/3 oz of the sugar and whisk until stiff and glossy.

• Fold in the remaining sugar and don't be too gentle, you need to dissolve the sugar.

• Place spoonfuls, large or small, on a baking sheet lined with non-stick paper and bake for about 1-1½ hours so they are set on the outside.

• How do you know when they are done? I'm afraid the only answer is to try one. Serve with the strawberries and cream.

Peaches with Lime and Ginger Cream

SERVES 4-6

300ml/10fl oz whipping cream
jar stem ginger and 4
   tablespoons of the syrup
4 limes
6 peaches, peeled destoned and
   cut into half-moon slices

Peaches certainly, but also nectarines, strawberries, pears, even rhubarb at an early spring picnic, go well with this flavoured cream.

• Whip the cream.

• Chop the ginger as finely as you can, a sticky job at the best of times.

• Grate the zest from the limes and combine the chopped ginger, ginger syrup and lime zest with the cream.

• Leave to sit for half an hour or so and serve with the peaches

Almond and Lemon Corn Cake

SERVES 8

125g/4oz butter, softened
125g/4oz caster sugar
zest of 2 lemons
2 medium-sized eggs, plus
    two egg yolks
75g/3 oz plain flour
100g/3½ oz whole blanched
    almonds
100g/3½ oz coarse polenta
    flour (not instant or quick-
    cook polenta)
2 teaspoons baking powder

Polenta cake, corn cake, call it what you will, the nutty flavour and gritty texture make this golden yellow cake a favourite pudding. Serve with a good scoop of creme fraiche, or with a pile of summer berries. If you have time for afternoon tea it slots in nicely, alongside a cup of best Darjeeling, but who has time for tea these days? Far better to serve it up at the end of a delicious picnic when you need something a little, but not too sweet.

You can buy ground almonds everywhere, but you will get a far better almond flavour if you buy whole blanched almonds and grind them yourself.

• Cream the butter and sugar together in a bowl along with the lemon zest and then beat in the eggs and egg yolks. Beat in the flour.

• Blitz the almonds in a food processor along with the polenta and baking powder and then beat into the lemon mixture.

• Pour into a 20cm/8 in cake tin and bake at 180°C/350°F/gas mark 4 for 45 minutes, or until the cake is cooked. Insert a skewer to test – the skewer will come out clean if the cake is cooked.

• Serve in slices.

Figs with Goat's Cheese Mascarpone

SERVES 4

8 figs
caster sugar
1 vanilla pod
125g/4 oz mascarpone
125g/4 oz fresh goat's
    cheese
150ml/5fl oz double cream

As with all fruit, there are good and not so good figs, but if I get a good one I remember it for days. The texture yes, but also the meatiness, and such a subtle sweetness. On holiday once in Italy there was a fig tree outside our Tuscan villa - at least that was how the brochure described our two-room apartment - where we would gather figs still warm from the evening sunshine. Being free, they had a particularly delicious edge.

- Cut the figs in a cross from top almost to the bottom and open out like a flower.

- Dust with caster sugar and grill until golden and bubbling.

- Meanwhile, split the vanilla pod and remove the seeds. (Put the vanilla pod in the bag of sugar to give it a subtle vanilla flavour.)

- Mix the seeds with both cheeses and the cream and beat to a smooth finish.

- Serve the figs with the goat's cheese mascarpone.

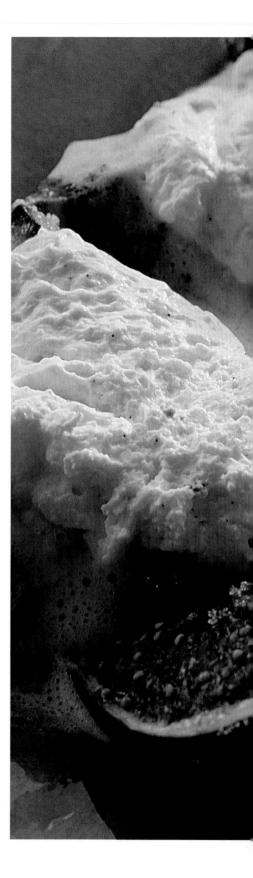

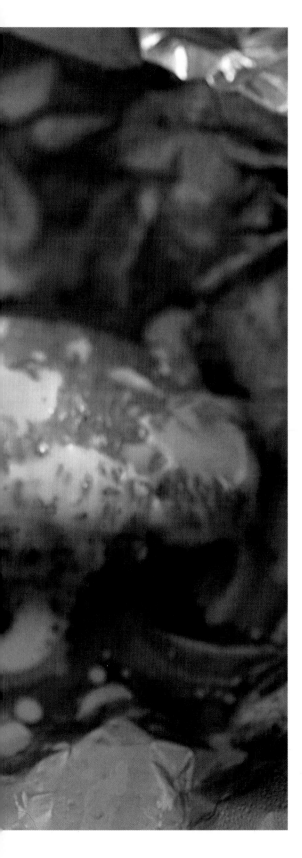

Baked Bananas with Cinnamon Butter and Brandy

SERVES 4

4 large bananas
soft dark brown sugar
butter
brandy
ground cinnamon
double cream or crème
fraîche

You have finished your picnic, the light is starting to fade and as you sit round the glowing embers of the fire the one thing missing is something sweet. A bar of chocolate – if it is a large one – may well do the trick, but try finishing with these bananas instead. Prepared at home, they can then be nestled into the dying embers.

• Peel the bananas and place each one in the middle of a piece of foil, large enough to accommodate the banana and other ingredients comfortably.

• Place a dessertspoon each of sugar, butter and brandy along with a generous pinch of cinnamon on top of each banana, wrap up tightly into a parcel and place in the fire.

• Take care when unwrapping, the steam is hot, but it smells fantastic. Serve with cream

Char-grilled Peaches, Honey and Yoghurt

SERVES 4

4-8 peaches, halved and
stoned
good runny honey, Greek
Greek, or Greek-style
yoghurt

Peaches char-grill particularly well. Not too much, just enough to give a slight edge, the sugars caramelised rather than burnt. Ripe specimens are essential, but then that goes without saying for all fruit. I once spent a few months living in the south of France and there families bought whole trays of peaches. Peach jam, peach compote, peach chutney – I for one cannot get enough of them.

• Char-grill the peaches until the bars of your barbecue have run sticky black lines across the cut sides of the peaches.

• Pile on to plates and serve with the honey and yoghurt.

Everlasting Syllabub

SERVES 4-6

8 tablespoons white wine or
  sherry
2 tablespoons brandy
pared zest and juice of 1 lemon
50g/2oz sugar
300ml/10fl oz double cream
nutmeg

This recipe comes from Elizabeth David, whose writings never cease to amuse, inform and stimulate. On syllabubs she traces their origins back to the 17th century, to parlour maids and streams of new, warm milk frothing up bowls of spiced cider or ale, a refreshing drink on a warm summer's day. This firmer version can be adjusted, altered and changed as you wish.

- Combine the first 3 ingredients in a bowl and leave overnight.

- Strain the liquid into a bowl and stir in the sugar until it has dissolved. Still stirring, pour in the cream slowly. Finally add a grating of nutmeg.

- Beat the syllabub with a wire whisk until it holds its shape - do not go on too long, or too vigorously, or the cream will curdle and separate into a buttery mass.

- Spoon the syllabub into small glasses or custard cups - there is enough for 4-6 people - and keep in a cool place (if possible, not in the refrigerator) for 2 days or more.

A few variations with syllabub

Rum to replace the brandy, lime to replace the lemon, cinnamon to replace the nutmeg, chopped nuts to sprinkle on top, or grated chocolate. Sherry works very well, try sake for a modern twist. Rose water too, makes for an Eastern flavour.

Fruit Fools

SERVES 4

500g/1lb fruit (rhubarb,
  gooseberries, strawberries,
  raspberries or blackberries)
50g/2 oz butter
sugar
300ml/10fl oz whipping cream

First it was the rhubarb, then we would move on to gooseberries, strawberries, then to raspberries and finally to blackberries. The year's fruit dressed up as a fool. My childhood is punctuated by my mother's and grandmother's commentary on the glut or otherwise of the fruit. Either it wasn't ripe, or it was all ripe together. Whichever way things happened to be, the question of what was for pudding became something of a standing joke. If the sun was shinning, it had to be fruit.

My favourite fool is gooseberry, their tart, very British taste a perfect foil for the cream - but most fruit is fantastic. If things are looking too sweet there is always lemon juice. A little alcohol never goes amiss. With the darker fools, keep a little of the fruit puree to decorate with at the end.

- Combine the prepared fruit and butter in a saucepan and cook over a gentle heat until it starts to collapse.

- Remove from the heat and mash with a fork, stirring in sugar to taste. Set aside to cool.

- Whip the cream and fold into the fruit puree once it has cooled.
Spoon into tall glasses, chill and serve.

Other fruits to fool

Plum, melon, peach, pineapple, orange, mango, blueberries.

Blackberry and Apple Charlotte

SERVES 4-6

750g/1lb 10oz cooking apples
sugar
250g/9oz blackberries
6 tablespoons butter
bread
1 bunch mint, finely chopped

Blackberry picking always reminds me of Ireland. The blackberries there are bigger, juicier and in every way better than anywhere else. What's more, there are more of them, easier to pick, cleaner. Do you detect the unashamedly biased view here? Along with the seemingly endless sunshine that accompanied our west of Ireland summers spent on empty golden beaches there was the ritual of blackberries. Everyone talked of the jam we would be enjoying, but in truth it was the pies I couldn't wait for.

My grandmother made the best pies ever. Baked in blue-lined enamel plates, the pastry was crunchy crisp, dusted with proper sugar and served with cream hand-milked up in the yard and made by my grandmother, who earlier in the day would have stood stooped on the scullery steps, skimming the cream from a large enamel bowl into a plain white jug. Second helpings were automatic as she sat back, a smoking cigarette in hand, her task of feeding us completed. My pastry has never been as good as hers, hence the charlotte recipe below.

• Peel, core and roughly chop the apples. Combine with 3 tablespoons of sugar in a saucepan and cook down over a gentle heat until you have a stiff puree.

• Add the blackberries, taste and add more sugar if necessary.

• Melt the butter and brush the inside of a 900g/2lb loaf tin with butter then and dust with sugar. Cut the crusts from the bread and, dipping each slice in the melted butter, line the loaf tin, ensuring there are no gaps.

• Add the mint to the apple and blackberry mixture and pour into the tin. Seal the top with more slices of bread dipped in butter.

• Bake in a preheated oven, 190°C/375°F/gas mark 5 for about 40 minutes, or until golden brown.

• Remove from the oven, allow to sit for 2 or 3 minutes, work a knife around the edge and turn out on to a large dish.

• Slice and serve with lots of cream.

Cherry Cake

MAKES ONE 20CM/8IN CAKE

150g/5oz butter, at room
    temperature
150g/5oz caster sugar
3 eggs
225g/8oz plain flour
1 teaspoon baking powder
300g/10oz glacé cherries
3 tablespoons ground almonds
grated zest of 2 lemons
450g/1lb stoned cherries
1 glass Pimms
tub of creme fraiche

A bowl of cherries, lip-gloss red or black and forbidding, is an early summer treat without compare. The flavour so delicate, the flesh deliciously crisp and refreshing. Flavour is all in a cherry, there is no fun if the crunch is unaccompanied. Buy well. In France, south of Lyon, cherry trees abound, the fruit increasingly shaken from trees as technology replaces people. These cherries are baked in enormous ovens with sugar to be shipped – Britain takes half the harvest – as glacé cherries. The destoning takes an age, but is worth it for the uninterrupted pleasure.

• Whisk the butter and sugar together until smooth. Lightly whisk the eggs and gently beat these into the butter mixture a spoonful at a time. Combine the flour and baking powder and sift this into the butter mixture, gradually folding it in.

• Roughly chop the glacé cherries and gently fold these in along with the almonds and lemon zest. Preheat the oven to 170°C/325°F/gas mark 3 and bake for 11/2 –2 hours.

• Combine the stoned cherries and Pimms and allow to soak. Serve with the cherry cake and the creme fraiche.

Drinks

Wine

Wine, as always, is probably the best, but there is no need to push the boat out. Outdoors is the place for good plonk. Leave your vintage claret for a grand dinner, the nuances of great burgundy for a special lunch. Something refreshing if it is white, gutsy if it is red. I used to dislike rosé, but in recent years I've changed my mind. If you are concerned about red and white drinkers it is a good compromise, both camps being satisfied. I am a devoted fan of sherry, a truly great wine vastly underpriced and of exceptional quality. The salty tang of a chilled manzanilla or fino is the perfect partner with seafood.

Beer

Refreshing and not too powerful. In recent years the whole idea of beer drinking has been given a new lease of life with the advent of micro beers. Look out for names like Hobgoblin, Freedom, Summer Lightening, these have depth, length and complexity, nothing like the bland pale imitation beer I grew up with. The same can be said of some of the Belgian, Czech and Bavarian beers now available. They put your average tin of froth to shame.

Non-alcoholic drinks

Old-fashioned home-made lemonade has to be one of the best. My grandmother always had a bottle in the fridge and it was sensational.

8 unwaxed lemons
225g/8oz caster sugar
2.5litres/4½ pints boiling water

• If you cannot get unwaxed lemons, scrub the waxed ones under hot water. Remove the lemon zest using a potato peeler. It is important not to remove the pith as this will make your lemonade bitter.

• Place the zest in a bowl with the sugar, pour over the boiling water, stir well to dissolve the sugar and allow to cool overnight. Once cool, strain, reserving the liquid and discarding the lemon zest.

• Squeeze the juice from the lemons, cover and place in the fridge.

• Combine the lemon juice with the reserved strained lemon water, chill and serve.

Tea and coffee

Tea keeps well over time while coffee deteriorates. Still it is rather chic to offer hot coffee at the end of an outdoor feast. In both cases keep the milk and sugar separate. And if you are having coffee, a slug of something warming is often surprisingly popular.

Iced tea and coffee may sound old fashioned but they are popular drinks in hot countries with reason, they are very refreshing. Add spices to either for variety, cloves for tea perhaps, cinnamon for coffee.

Other drinks

Pimms is a popular summer drink, but with all the paraphernalia associated with it in the form of mint and fruit salad it's a bit cumbersome for long journeys.

Cider, particularly some of the Normandy and unpasteurised ciders. As a child we used to have an Irish brand called Bulmers, which in those days came in dark, stone-stoppered bottles. A delight.

In India the big question was whether you drank your lassi sweet (you were probably from the north) or salty (probably from the south). Both make fine and refreshing drinks, the salt giving it a more adult flavour. Mix equal quantities of plain yoghurt and water with mint and salt or sugar to taste. Chill and serve.

Marinades

2 garlic cloves, peeled
1 dessertspoon cumin seeds

pinch of cayenne powder

Blitz everything in a processor, or grind in a pestle and mortar and coat the steaks in the mixture, leaving to marinate overnight. Brush off and grill until cooked.

6 tablespoons plain yoghurt
1 dessertspoon ground cumin seeds
2 teaspoons ground coriander
1 teaspoon paprika

pinch of cayenne pepper
1 garlic clove, peeled and crushed
a generous grinding of black pepper

Combine all the ingredients and coat the meat well. Leave to marinate overnight. Brush off and grill until cooked.

1 dessertspoon sherry vinegar
2 tablespoons sherry
1 garlic clove, peeled and finely chopped

1 tablespoon finely chopped shallot
1 teaspoon dried thyme
4 tablespoons olive oil

Combine all the ingredients and coat the meat well. Leave to marinate overnight.

For spare ribs or chicken wings
(for 500g/1lb spare ribs or chicken wings)

4 garlic cloves, finely chopped
1 tablespoon finely chopped coriander root
1 tablespoon oyster sauce
1 tablespoon soy sauce

1 tablespoon fish sauce
1 dessertspoon sugar
500g/1 lb chicken wings

Mix all the ingredients together and coat the spare ribs or chicken wings. Set aside for at least one hour, two is better, covered with cling film. Barbecue or grill until cooked.

Marinade for steaks, chops and fish cutlets
(for 4 steaks)

1 heaped teaspoon dried thyme
8 tablespoons olive oil
3 tablespoons vinegar

chilli flakes
6 peppercorns, crushed
1 garlic clove, finely chopped

Combine all the marinade ingredients, coat the meat well and leave for 30 minutes to 1 hour, turning frequently. If you are marinating fish, use 1tablespoon of vinegar and allow 15 minutes instead of 30. Brush off and grill until cooked.

Variations: use different herbs: bay leaves, fennel seeds, oregano. Vinegars can also provide variety: red and white wine, sherry, balsamic or even Japanese rice vinegar. Or you can use a different source of acid; lemon, lime, pineapple, grapefruit.

Marsala marinade

This is a favourite marinade, which can be used to coat any meat or fish, from a salmon cutlet to a whole leg of lamb.

1 teaspoon ground coriander
1 teaspoon ground cumin
1 teaspoon paprika
1 teaspoon ground ginger

pinch of chilli powder
pinch of turmeric
vegetable oil

Mix everything together and combine with enough oil to form a paste. Use to coat the meat/fish. Grill until cooked.

Tamarind marinade

This marinade gives a gloriously subtle and exotic flavour to game, fish and beef.

4 chillies, deseeded and chopped
2 tablespoons finely chopped shallots
3 garlic cloves, peeled and chopped
2.5cm/1 in piece of galangal or fresh root ginger, peeled and finely chopped
4 lime leaves, finely sliced
2 sticks of lemon grass, the dry outside leaves discarded and the inside finely sliced
2 walnut-sized pieces of tamarind soaked and squeezed
2 tablespoons vegetable oil

Blitz all the ingredients in a blender, season with salt and pepper and cook for 10 minutes in a small saucepan. Allow to cool and use with your chosen meat or fish. Grill until cooked.

For steaks, game and rabbit

1 onion, finely chopped
1 glass of brandy
1 bay leaf, chopped

1 bunch parsley stalks, roughly chopped
olive oil
6 allspice, basked with a rolling pin

Combine all the ingredients and use to coat the meat. Grill until cooked.

For fish

generous pinch of saffron soaked in warm water
1 garlic clove, mashed with salt to form a paste

1 tablespoon chopped parsley
juice of a lemon

Combine all the ingredients, season with salt and pepper and use to coat the fish. Grill until cooked

Salad Dressings and Mayonnaise

I tend to vary salad dressings by varying the oil and vinegar I use. My wife is keen on balsamic, so I use that quite a lot. My own preference is for an aged wine vinegar. Rice vinegar is also good, as is sherry or cider vinegar. Lemon juice is often a welcome change, as is lime juice. For olive oil, you need a directory and large wallet – I try to taste before I buy. If I can in 5-litre cans. You generally pay the bottle price for 4 litres, the fifth one being free. Which is good for me as I use gallons, or should I say litres.

Other salad dressing ideas
A little tarragon with a green salad in summer is refreshing.
Mustard is a good addition, particularly with the more bitter leaves; rocket, mustard, watercress.
   If you are using garlic, make sure it is mashed to a puree with a little salt, which makes it more digestible.
   Walnut oil makes for a change, but tends to be very strong, dilute with a flavourless oil.
Toasted sesame seed oil falls into the same category as walnut oil.

Mayonnaise

2 egg yolks
300ml/10fl oz light olive oil
salt
lemon juice to taste

Place the egg yolks in bowl and while continuously stirring, add the oil drop by drop advancing to a steady stream as the mixture emulsifys. Season with salt and lemon juice to taste. If, half way through, the mixture becomes too stiff to whisk, add a few drops of lemon juice.

Index